THE SOUTHERN WAY

GW00675734

CONTENTS

© Kevin Robertson (Noodle Books) and the various contributors 2010

ISBN 978-1-906419-30-1

First published in 2010 by Kevin Robertson

under the **NOODLE BOOKS** imprint

PO Box 279

Corhampton

SOUTHAMPTON

SO32 3ZX

www.noodlebooks.co.uk

Printed in England by

Ian Allan Printing Ltd

Hersham, Surrey

Continuing the theme of 'Road Vehicles' briefly - see page 48 of this issue, these two delightful images appeared recently. The first is purported to be at Nine Elms, is this a vehicle with trailer or an early 'ro-ro' design? The bottom view is far easier, a Basingstoke built Thorneycroft complete with solid tyres. Vehicles of this type date from around the WW1 period and yet clearly continued in use for some time.

Editorial Introduction

A definite narrow gauge theme to this issue, but even so with two distinct comments. Firstly the topic of the Middlebere Tramway should not seen as referring just to the narrow gauge line in Purbeck. Instead the author has carefully and cleverly placed the line in context with what was happening elsewhere relative to rail communication. It makes for a fascinating account although you will have to wait for at least one more issue to complete the full story.

Our second narrow gauge item concerns Porton. This is perhaps a fairly well known system although I am certain some of the views will be new to most. (Wonderful archives are often to be found amongst the various local history groups and societies.) Whilst we may look at Porton from a railway and archaeological perspective, it must not be forgotten that it was the advent of chemical warfare that was responsible for its construction. I have driven past the site of the railway many times in recent months, although there is little if anything much left to see nowadays. In the same area was the line from Newton Tony Junction to Amesbury and Bulford, once seriously intended to connect with the MSWJ at Tidworth. Nearby was also the line from the GWR Codford to the army camp nearby.

The subject of one of these military routes, that to Amesbury and Bulford once of the last survivors, would make for a fascinating study. (A broad hint here which I am delighted to say has already been taken up.) We would be delighted also to hear about other military lines serving the Southern area and about which there is information and preferably photographs.

Of late it has been a privilege to receive a quantity of material relative to the careers of several former Southern men. One of these may perhaps be known to some, Allan Cobb, who retired in 1945 from the position of Running Superintendent to OVS Bulleid. A major piece on his career is in the process of preparation for a future issue. Do please though keep things coming: I do have pangs of guilt when something is perhaps not used as rapidly as would be desirable, but we do try and use things in rotation.

Aside from articles for 'SW', I can also confirm several books that are in preparation for late 2010 and beyond. I like to think that the model market and likewise the book market feed on each other to some extend, a new model may lead to a book on the topic and vice versa. Sometimes we even manage to tie in similar release dates although both types of material are likely to require varying degrees of preparation.

Thanks to one of our regular proof readers we also now have a set of writers guidelines available, the intention being that we all work to a common standard. These are available by e-mail free of charge. If you are in the process of, or planning; a contribution please let us know, a copy is easily sent.

I am also grateful to all who responded to my recent 'fishing expedition' in a recent issue over the production of an annual. The overwhelming response was to keep with 'Special' issues. I bow to your request.

Front Cover - *Halcyon days at Ventnor West. Set No 503. The vehicle is an arc-roof former LBSCR vehicle. The vehicle is likely to be either No. 4169 or 6367. These were reported as transferred to the Isle of Wight in 1938 and were used on Ventnor West trains up to closure. In Mike King's 'An Illustrated History of Southern Pull-Push Stock', there is a b/w illustration of this set in April 1949, reported as freshly outshopped in malachite green. Could it be that the colour should have been the red seen here? The view was taken shortly before closure in 1952.*

Paul Hersey collection

Rear Cover - *Continuing the C2X theme, 32522 is recorded at Ashford not long before its demise in 1961.*

Pages 2/3 - The unmistakable outline of Exmouth Junction, with 21C106 'Bude' with original short smoke deflectors, being made ready for work 14 November 1945, at which time it was only a very few months old. The distinctive extra long smoke deflectors later carried by this engine were fitted in 1948 ready for the interchange trails of that year.

AN APPEAL

In connection with something rather special planned for later this year, we are urgently seeking colour views of Bulleid coaches - all types, running in BR service. Any assistance would be much appreciated.

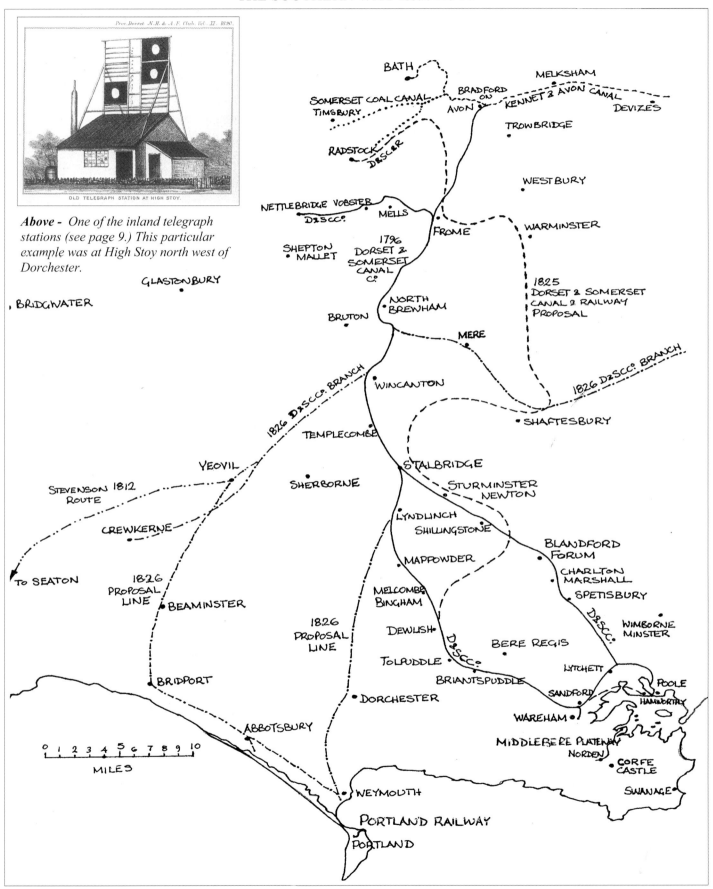

Prov. Dorset N.H. & A.F. Club. Vol. XI. 1890.

OLD TELEGRAPH STATION AT HIGH STOY.

Above - *One of the inland telegraph stations (see page 9.) This particular example was at High Stoy north west of Dorchester.*

BATH

MELKSHAM

BRADFORD ON AVON

SOMERSET COAL CANAL
TIMSBURY

KENNET & AVON CANAL

DEVIZES

TROWBRIDGE

RADSTOCK

D&SC&R

WESTBURY

NETTLEBRIDGE VOBSTER
D&SCC?.

MELLS

FROME

WARMINSTER

SHEPTON MALLET

1796
DORSET & SOMERSET CANAL C?

1825
DORSET & SOMERSET CANAL & RAILWAY PROPOSAL

GLASTONBURY

, BRIDGWATER

NORTH BREWHAM

BRUTON

MERE

1826 D&SCC? BRANCH

WINCANTON

1826 D&SCC?. BRANCH

SHAFTESBURY

TEMPLECOMBE

YEOVIL

STEVENSON 1812 ROUTE

STALBRIDGE

SHERBORNE

STURMINSTER NEWTON

CREWKERNE

LYNDLINCH
SHILLINGSTONE

BLANDFORD FORUM

TO SEATON

1826 PROPOSAL LINE

MAPPOWDER

CHARLTON MARSHALL

SPETISBURY

BEAMINSTER

MELCOMBE BINGHAM

DEWLISH

BERE REGIS

D&SCC?

WIMBORNE MINSTER

1826 PROPOSAL LINE

TOLPUDDLE

D&SCC?

LYTCHETT

BRIDPORT

DORCHESTER

BRIANTSPUDDLE

SANDFORD

POOLE

HAMWORTHY

WAREHAM

ABBOTSBURY

MIDDLEBERE PLATEWAY
NORDEN

0 1 2 3 4 5 6 7 8 9 10
MILES

WEYMOUTH

CORFE CASTLE

SWANAGE

PORTLAND RAILWAY

PORTLAND

THE MIDDLEBERE PLATEWAY

Its History and Connections with the Early Railways of Southern England

Peter Hollins

Origins

It is rumoured that Napoleon Bonaparte once landed at Lulworth - in order to survey the Purbeck coastline for a suitable invasion site. This is probably as close as he physically came to a railway in Dorset, however his political influence helped shape the early railway developments along the south coast of Britain as illustrated by this article.

This then is the story of how Dorset's railways were born, and how the building of a Georgian horse-drawn mineral tramway evolved into the construction of a network of main lines, linking most towns in Dorset with London and the North by 1874.

Dorset's first railway, the Middlebere Plateway, was constructed a year after the battle of Trafalgar, to serve the Norden clay pits near Corfe Castle. Although it remained an isolated curiosity for almost the whole of the next 100 years, the key people behind the ball clay industry it served all became involved in the creation of the local rail network during the first half of the 19th century.

Whilst Dorset's first railway opened during this period, its concept can be traced back long before the Napoleonic era to 1725. The Pitt family were the landlords of Norden Farm and clay mines during Napoleonic times, but also had previous experience of railway construction and operation in Durham. The family had originated in Blandford, Dorset, but by the mid 18th century had spread out to Stratfield Saye (in Berkshire), Kingston Maurward, Encombe, Arne and elsewhere by the mid 18th century.

George Pitt of Stratfield Saye was prospecting in the 1720s and became the owner of Tanfield Moor Colliery in Durham. It was he who financed the building of a branch of the Tanfield Waggonway in 1728 to transport coal from the pits to the staithes at Dunston on the banks of the River Tyne.

This Colliery and its 4 ft. gauge wooden waggonway passed down to John Pitt of Kingston Maurward, and then to William Moreton Pitt his son, who also inherited the Encombe estate in 1787: this included Norden Farm and clay pits.

William Pitt's cousin, Lord Rivers of Stratfield Saye, was the landowner of the Arne clay pits, and also owned most of the land in the Stoborough area, south of Wareham.

In 1840 the Pike Brothers built their tramway passing through Stoborough on the way from their clay pits at Furzebrook to Ridge Wharf on the Frome.

The Pitt family were also friends with Ralph Allen of Prior Park in Bath, especially William Pitt the elder, cousin of George Pitt. From his workings at Combe Down, Ralph Allen supplied Bath stone to George Pitt's Stratfield Saye House, as well as many prestigious buildings in London and Bath.

In 1730 Ralph Allen built his wooden waggonway to transport stone from his quarries in Combe Down to Dolemead Wharf on the river Avon. From Dolemead stone could be shipped to any port in the country and also across the river into the city of Bath. He is also credited with improving the wagon brake, which is not surprising as the land from Prior Park rises steeply away from the Avon towards Combe Down, with an average gradient of 1 in 16.

Replica of a Tanfield coal chaldron.

Causey Arch on the Tanfield Waggonway.

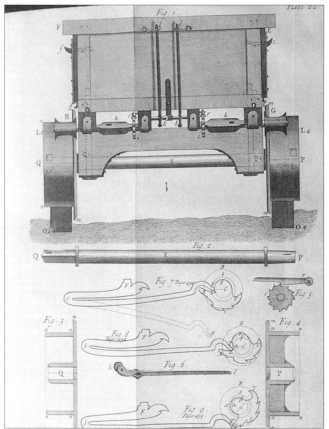

Drawings of Ralph Allen's Stone Waggons by Charles de Labelaye, 1734.

Ralph Allen used the wooden waggonways of the Newcastle area as his starting point, and engaged the Bristol engineer John Padmore to vastly improve on the design of the Newcastle wagons for his Prior Park railway. It is possible that George Pitt's Tanfield Waggonway might have been the inspiration for Ralph Allen's improved version in Bath, as this was the largest and most heavily engineered waggonway in the country at the time.

The stone waggons were equipped with brass axel (*sic*) bearings, ratchet operated independent four wheel braking and free wheeling at one end of each axle to cope with sharp bends at the bottom of the incline. Each wagon carried about 4 tons of stone, was constructed of oak and iron with cast iron wheels and cost £30 to build in 1730.

Despite the sophistication of the wagons, the wooden rails appear to have lacked any form of cross ties and relied on being buried in the ballast to maintain the gauge. A single-track line was built, but there were no points, unlike the Tanfield Waggonway which boasted three tracks at its busiest section. Plateway points were said to have been invented by Richard Fothergill of the Tredegar Iron Works - during a sermon one Sunday towards the end of the 18th Century!

At Combe Down, loaded stone wagons were sent down the incline by gravity with one man controlling the brakes, the empties worked back up from Dolemead Wharf by a pair of horses.

Unfortunately most of the technical advances of Allen's waggonway were lost when the line was closed and the equipment auctioned off shortly after his death in 1764.

Two things Ralph Allen's Prior Park railway did have in common with Fayle's tramway at Norden were the unusual track gauge of 3ft. 9in., and the use of low friction axle bearings. As an aside, Ralph Allen's other claim to fame was the modernization of the Post Office with the introduction of the cross post services. This, together with the work of his successor, John Palmer, in introducing the fast mail coach services, paved the way for coach operators such as Chaplin, who by the 1830s operated a huge fleet of vehicles across the country. In 1836 the South Western Railway proposed an extension west from Basingstoke to Salisbury, Exeter, Plymouth and Falmouth, with a branch to Barnstaple - this was the exact same route as Chaplin's mail coaches were plying in 1836.

As is well known, with victory over Napoleon's army in 1815, the Duke of Wellington was presented with the Stratfield Saye estate from a grateful nation, the Government having purchased the estate from Lord Rivers in 1817 and presented it to the Duke.

The Duke's first intention was to demolish the existing manor house and build his own Waterloo Palace in its place. In the event this did not come to fruition as the project proved too expensive. Had he succeeded, would Basingstoke station even have been called Waterloo?

Luckily for the South Western the same fate did not befall Waterloo Bridge, or the London terminus might have been called the 'Cow Shed' after the previous building on that site, or 'The Rising Sun' after the adjacent public house. (Ref. C. Hamilton-Ellis, *The South Western Railway*).

But at the start of the 19th century, there was general uncertainty over national security and with it financial investment. Thus many projected transport schemes simply vanished overnight with little or nothing being constructed. These included the Dorset & Somerset Canal and the London & Portsmouth Iron Railway.

A brief respite in the hostilities with France promoted further new-build speculation, but this enthusiasm was cut short in 1803 when war was again declared between Britain and France. Elaborate measures were then taken to defend the country against potential invasion along the channel coast, including an evacuation plan for the coastal regions and an extensive telegraph network.

It was during the Napoleonic wars that William Moreton Pitt and William Clavell were involved with a scheme for the evacuation of the residents of the Isle of Purbeck in the event of French invasion. This included the allocation of escape routes for personnel and livestock, which one would imagine involved the waggonways and various quays in use for shipping clay and stone. Troops to be mustered in the event of an invasion were volunteer reserves, one of whom was Lieutenant Joseph Willis - who later became tenant of Norden Farm and manager of the clay pits.

Again as part of the preparations for the impending French invasion, was construction of a line of telegraph stations, parallel to the south coast, intended to cover an area between Plymouth, Dover and London. These telegraph stations were mounted on top of hills and relied on a series of cable operated shutters to give a visual signal to the next station. Could this even be where the idea of South Western Railway disc signals came from?

Further signal stations were set up at strategic positions along the coast, such as St. Aldham's Head (more usually known today as St. Alban's Head) and Ballard Down. From here beacons were used to signal inland and semaphore flags to signal to ships out to sea. Similar flag-signaling was used at Middlebere Quay and Newton in Victorian times, this time to communicate with the clay barges then plying across Poole Harbour.

Following construction of the Middlebere Plateway in 1806, it was hoped that production and thus profits from the clay pits would increase rapidly. Unfortunately for William Moreton Pitt, the continuing hostilities in Europe did not allow the increase in clay production he had hoped for and in 1807 he had to sell the Encombe estate to pay off some of his loans. This was purchased by John Scott, the Lord Chancellor, later the 1st Lord Eldon.

In 1823 William Moreton Pitt saw another investment opportunity and bought Swanage with a view to turning it into another popular sea-side town like Weymouth. Accordingly in 1826 coal from his Tanfield colliery was being shipped to Swanage: in later years coal was shipped to Swanage via Hamworthy Quay and the LSWR. A few years later in 1842, the LSWR was using Tanfield Moor coal in their coking plant based a quarter of a mile from Nine Elms, probably because Tanfield coal is a very good coking coal.

Unfortunately for William Pitt, Swanage did not grow as fast as he had expected and his income was less than his expenditure. The rapid growth of Swanage as a seaside watering-place eventually occurred subsequent to the arrival of the LSWR in 1885. Although some growth of the town must have occurred by 1827, as Lord Eldon writes to his brother "...we are getting a nuisance here at Swanage, of a bathing place of much resort....and now I can't spend my time at inns, when I am out of town". His quiet Purbeck retreat was being invaded by visitors.

In 1838 the Norden Farm and clay pits and also the Tanfield Colliery, were sold off from the Pitt estate in order to clear the outstanding debts following the death of William Moreton Pitt in 1836. Norden Farm and clay pits were bought by John Scott, the second Lord Eldon of Encombe, only weeks after his grandfather's death.

Another early Dorset railway influenced more by Georgian architectural fashion than economic climate, was the Merchant's Railway on Portland. King George III paid frequent visits to Weymouth and on one visit he called on William Moreton Pitt at Kingston Maurward and passed the derogatory commented about the residence, "brick, Pitt, brick". Following this, in 1794 Kingston Maurward was entirely clad in Portland stone at Pitt's expense.

Built to transport stone from the quarries down to the quay at Castletown, the Portland Railway was constructed using stone block sleepers and edge rail to a gauge of 4' 6". Opened in 1825, the Portland Railway was Dorset's first public railway but the second line to open in the county. The third was Pike's tramway from Furzebrook to Ridge; the fourth being the Southampton and Dorchester. This was then followed by the Wilts Somerset and Weymouth line and then numerous pottery tramways during the 1850s.

Although there is no evidence that William Pitt had any influence on this railway, he was on the board of trade for Portland and knew the quarry men from the work he had had done on Kingston Maurward.

Two other transport schemes in the south were also to become victims of the Napoleonic influence, one being the Surrey Iron Railway (SIR), the other the ill-fated Dorset and Somerset Canal and Railway. Both of these projects were eventually literally buried, in part at least, under LSWR permanent way.

The SIR was thought to have influenced Benjamin Fayle, the London merchant running the Purbeck clay mines, to construct the Middlebere Plateway in 1806. John Hodgkinson who engineered the Middlebere Plateway, worked with SIR chief engineer William Jessop on numerous projects, as he had with Benjamin Outram, his cousin and Jessop's business partner. John Hodgkinson was working with William Jessop on the Caerleon Bridge in 1805, only months before starting work

B. Fayle & Co. offices, Carpenters shop and Blacksmiths at Norden, c1900. The Plateway runs from left to right in front of the buildings. New Line Farm is in the background. The LSWR Swanage Branch was to the left.   *B Buxton collection*

on the Middlebere Plateway. Jessop was otherwise occupied at that time as he was building the Bristol Floating Docks.

Started as a scheme to ship coal by canal from the Somerset collieries to Poole Harbour, the Dorset and Somerset Canal and Railway ended up as a much more grandiose and consequently even less achievable scheme, after the intervention of some influential Dorset investors.

The promoters of the proposed railway between Poole and North Somerset included John Calcraft, owner of the clay pits at Threshers and Newton as well as estates in Somerset; William Ponsonby, whose Canford estate encompassed the southern end of the line including Hamworthy and the town of Poole (he later became chairman of the Southampton and Dorchester Railway); George Penney, a Poole merchant, a Quaker and the local agent for B. Fayle & Co. of Norden; and latterly, Thomas Wanhill, Mayor of Poole and agent for the Lake clay pits in Hamworthy.

The Surrey Iron Railway

Started in 1801 with an authorised capital of £50,000, the Surrey Iron Railway was intended to convey the products of Croydon and the Wandle Valley to Wandsworth basin on the Thames from where they could be shipped into the City. Some of the produce carried in this way was timber, copper, iron, bricks, beer, charcoal, stone, lime, grain and flour.

On 8th June 1802 it was reported that amongst many others, the 'Portsmouth Wagon' weighing 8 to 10 tons and pulled by 8 horses, passed over the rails to Wandsworth, without mishap or damage to the track. Completed in 1803 by William Jessop, the line followed the construction principles and preferred 4' 2" gauge of Benjamin Outram. It was shortly followed by construction of the Croydon, Merstham and Godstone Iron Railway, which extended the line southwards to Merstham.

At a meeting of shareholders in August 1803, it was resolved unanimously to construct an extension from Merstham to Portsmouth and from Wandsworth into the City of London, this by raising £400,000 in shares. The new venture was to be called The London and Portsmouth Iron Railway, the intention being to provide a route from London to the important Naval port of Portsmouth. Goods and men could then be transported direct, avoiding the Straits of Dover and such parts of the English Channel most vulnerable to attack from the French Navy.

Had Napoleon's Navy not been defeated, the Portsmouth direct line would certainly have been a plateway built in the reign of George III: the railway had already been surveyed by William Jessop prior to the battle of Trafalgar.

Following Trafalgar, French naval activity decreased and goods reverted to being transported by coastal shipping. The intended extension of the 'iron railway' to Portsmouth and London was destined never to be built. After 1815 and the cessation of hostilities in Europe, the economic climate also changed and with the added competition from the now complete Croydon canal, the Surrey Iron Railway went into decline. A later description of this line given as, "a miserable team of donkeys, crawling at a rate of 4 mph, with several trucks of stone and lime behind them". Eventually after negotiations with the London and South Western, the SIR was sold in 1844 for £19,000. It was at this stage that the route of the SIR was surveyed by Joseph Locke with a view to converting it to steam operation. It was, though, found unsuitable and sold again by the LSWR, this time to the London and Brighton Railway, at cost. The final closure of the SIR came on Monday 31st August 1846.

This first public railway can also boast two other achievements. In August 1803, a model of the proposed iron railway was placed in the Swan Inn, Chichester, for public inspection. Thus might this claim to have been the world's first model railway? Then in September 1905, long, of course, after the LBSCR had bought the CM & G railway, one of the fairly rare murders on a railway took place in Merstham tunnel, where the body of Mary Sophia Money was found. The identity of her killer was never discovered, and the case remains unsolved to this day.

The Dorset and Somerset Canal and Railway Company

In 1768 it was proposed that a canal should be constructed to effectively cut off the south-western peninsula of England and so provide coastal cargoes with a short cut between Liverpool, Bristol and London via the Kennet and Avon. Canal. Additionally it was to provide a passage from the Somerset coal fields to the south coast and beyond.

So it was that in 1793, the Dorset and Somerset Canal became one of several proposed routes to provide this short cut for coastal shipping between London and Bristol. The others ventures were: The Bristol & English Channels Ship Canal, The Bristol & English Channels Junction Canal, The Grand Western Canal - from the river Exe at Topsham to the river Tone at Taunton, and the Southampton and Salisbury Canal, the latter having with a proposed extension from Salisbury to Wilcot (near Pewsey) and via the Kennet & Avon to Bath. Evidently the merchants of Bristol must have been keen to see a short cut in operation, as 40 from the 89 initial subscribers to the Southampton and Salisbury Canal lived in Bristol.

Construction of a canal between Nettlebridge (between Shepton Mallet and Radstock) in the Somerset coal fields, and the Dorset coast was authorised by 36 George III Cap 47: 24th March 1796, with an estimated cost of £146,008.

CM & G. Track Preserved at Merstham.

Work commenced in September 1796.

On the neighbouring Somerset Coal Canal, Weldon's caisson locks were going to be used on the steeply graded parts of the navigation. Unfortunately, despite a successful demonstration being given to the Prince of Wales, this form of lock proved impossible to maintain in working condition.

In 1800 Benjamin Outram was called in to find a solution. He recommended the use of the Fussell system of balanced locks and inclined plane tramways for the hills on the path of the Somerset Coal Canal.

The D & S C Co. also followed these recommendations, Fussell's locks were incorporated into their canal at Mells near Frome, whilst the first Fussell balanced lock had been successfully tried out at public demonstration in 1800.

In his patent, James Fussell, an Iron Founder of Mells, did not restrict his balanced water system to canal locks alone, but included this in the use of inclined plane tramways: such as was used on the Lynton and Lynmouth cliff lift.

A further Act of 1803 was sought to raise funds as well as to incorporate additional features, as most of the initial funding had already been spent on building part of the short branch from Frome to Nettlebridge.

The amended Act gave the promoters the right to construct part of the canal route as a 'Rail-Way' where required, but again the outbreak of war with France put the project on hold with no further funds forthcoming. With the announcement of hostilities, James Fussell, no doubt realising the business opportunity this presented to his iron works, immediately offered to supply the British army with pikes made in his works. (It is not reported if the Government availed themselves of this offer.)

The D&SCCo. was recorded as being abandoned by 1811, officially due to the hostilities with France, although in reality more through overspending and lack of capital. In January 1826, the remaining shareholders eventually resigned themselves to turning the project into a railway, by which time also the emphasis had moved to shipping coal from Somerset to Poole Harbour. Poole's existing supply of coal then came mainly from the north of England by coaster and was thus susceptible to disruption by bad weather at sea.

On November 26 1825, at the Red Lion in Wareham,

Left - Setting stone sleepers using wooden track gauges prior to laying plates.
Bottom - Cast iron plates are nailed to the stone sleepers using double headed wrought iron spikes into an oak sleve, set into a pre-drilled hole in each sleeper.

Opposite page, top - Middlebere Plateway stone sleeper.
Bottom Trackbed of the Middlebere Plateway near the Arne Road Crossing in 2006. Moderate earthworks ensured a gentle falling gradient from Norden to Middlebere Quay.

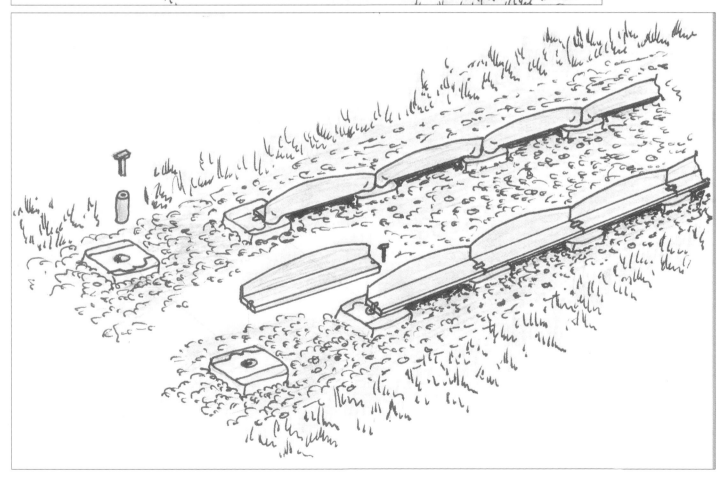

a Meeting chaired by J. Calcraft M.P. proposed a rival railway scheme to replace the dormant Dorset & Somerset Canal Co., to run from Radstock to Poole via Blackmore Vale and Bere Regis, terminating at Penney's shipyard in Hamworthy. There would also be a branch from Sandford Bridge to Wareham. The estimated cost was £300,000 for 80 miles of line.

Mr. Ponsonby, Mr. Rutter and Capt. Whalley were in favour of the scheme, but J. Frampton in opposition. Mr. Bayly stated there would be opposition from existing shareholders of the D & S Co., and suggested that the original company be re-invested to promote the railway.

In January 1826 a meeting of the original shareholders resolved to fund construction of the railway, starting from Frome and by utilising the partly finished canal bed. From that point they would extend south towards Shillingstone, with branches to serve Crewkerne and Salisbury off the main route.

A meeting was held in February 1826 at the George Inn, Frome, under the chairmanship of Thomas S Bailward, to discuss re-financing the old D & S C Co. and to complete the line as a railway, in place of a canal, and to quell the rival scheme being promoted in Dorset. It was stated that the Bristol Channel to Basingstoke Railway would cross and then run parallel to the D & S C Co. line, and a branch of the D & S C Co.

would be executed from Radstock to Vobster to serve the coal pits in that area. The railway would be constructed on the part finished Frome branch, then extended south to Sturminster as funds permitted. Projected branch lines could be built to Mere, Hindon, Salisbury and Shaftesbury, and Sherborne, Crewkerne

HOW TO BUILD A PLATEWAY - Opposite page: *"Follow the marked line of the track, placing dressed stone block sleepers at 3 feet intervals along the line. Space the stone blocks by using track gauges placed into the pre-drilled holes in the sleepers, and pack round with gravel ballast to secure in place, using a mason's level on top of the blocks to ensure the sleepers are vertically in line. Insert oak treenails (plug) into the holes in sleepers, then place cast iron plate rail between sleepers with notched ends in line with centre of sleeper holes. Hammer iron spike into treenail between aligned ends of rails, until the head is flush with the running surface."*

and Yeovil, all to serve as outlets for the Somerset coal. 7,000 tons of coal a week was projected to be transported on the new line. Messrs. Tredgold and Bennett estimated it would cost £16,000 to construct the Frome branch line on the existing canal base, and £24,000 to complete the line to Wincanton. The proposals were passed unanimously, but no more was published after this meeting.

Had it been built at this time, it is probable the line would have been laid to edge rail, rather than being constructed as a plateway, as one of the consulting engineers was the forward thinking Thomas Tredgold, who viewed plateways as inefficient and inferior to edge rail with flanged wheels.

The poor economic climate of Britain at the time, and the death of one of the promoters prevented any further progress and the project was shelved once more.

In May 1826 the Bristol and Bath Railroad Company was also dissolved for economic reasons, the excess funds donated to "the distressed weavers of the North of England".

On January 18th 1843, an article in the Dorset County Chronicle lamented the demise of the Dorset and Somerset Canal and Railway Co., which was laid aside following the death of the eminent Iron Founder (although not named as such, this was probably a reference to James Fussell) from Somerset, who had been the main promoter.

Meanwhile a survey for a line from Glastonbury to the English Channel had been carried out at this period, with Poole selected as the most desirable port on the south coast. This latest scheme was for a railway from Bridgewater to Poole via Langport, Ilchester, Yeovil, Sherborne, Sturminster and Blandford.

The Dorset & Somerset scheme was revived again in 1844 as the Bristol and English Channels Junction Railway, with Thomas Wanhill, Richard Pinney, G Parrott, J Gosse and George Penney as promoters, all members of Poole council who were also responsible for the management of Poole Harbour.

In a meeting of Poole Council on 18 June 1844, it was resolved that the scheme would benefit the harbour, therefore some of the Council's Quay funds were allocated to carry out the preliminary arrangements for promotion of the railway, and adverts were placed in the Salisbury & Winchester Journal and the Dorset County Chronicles.

In December 1846 William Pike was accompanied by George Penney of B. Fayle & Co. and John Brown of Wareham, in the promotion of the Bristol & Poole Railway. At one meeting Pike states that he had conversed with George Stephenson about the transportation of clay by rail, whilst studying the feasibility of setting up potteries in Birmingham. Stephenson had told him that a charge of 3½d per ton was made with an additional half-farthing for the truck.

Charles Castleman's brother, Edward Castleman, another member of the prominent family of Wimborne solicitors who promoted the Southampton and Dorchester Railway, negotiated with the GWR and the LSWR on behalf of the company, but with no success as the GWR were backing the WS&W line and the LSWR were proposing a line from the S&DR at Wim-

borne via Blandford to Bruton and were not wanting the expense of building a line any further north through the hilly parts of north Somerset.

The arguments for and against the railway hinged around the effect on the trade through Poole Harbour, by 1846 primarily that of the clay. The loss of this trade was being balanced by the use of Poole for export of manufactured goods from the North and coal from Somerset.

Mr. Parrott even refers to his involvement with the failed 1825 scheme over much the same route and its abandonment due to a construction cost of £2,000,000: more than double the cost of the Liverpool & Manchester Railway.

Understandably, without firm backing from any of the existing railway companies, the B & E C J R lost out to rival schemes in the area which were backed by either the GWR or the LSWR.

Shortly afterwards in 1847, following the success of both the Southampton and Dorchester Railway and the Wilts Somerset and Weymouth, it was decided at a meeting chaired by W. Ponsonby, that a Blandford branch from Wimborne on the Southampton and Dorchester Railway should be built with the financial backing of the LSWR. This branch line was to connect with a branch of the Wilts Somerset and Weymouth from Bruton to Blandford, and thus replace the failed B&ECJR. No mention is given of the change of gauge at Blandford, perhaps potential investors were more shrewd as finance was never forthcoming.

In 1852 another attempt was made to revive the Poole to Bristol route, this time with J.J. Guest of Canford leading the promotion of 'The South Midland Union Railway', and with William Pike as one of the directors. This scheme almost exactly described the 1874 S & D J R route via Bath, forming a junction with the Midland Railway at Mangotsfield. John Guest's death at the end of 1852 postponed this attempt until the end of 1853, when it was revived but with the route shortened to Bruton. At this period there was also move to connect with the Somerset scheme to construct a line to Burnham on Sea.

Had the D & S C & R actually been built, it would have beaten the Liverpool and Manchester Railway to being the first major cross country route. The D & S C & R could also have had Royal patronage, as one of Napoleon's successors, the exiled Charles X and his entourage, landed at Poole in August 1830 and were taken to Lulworth Castle. There was also mention of steam haulage and passenger services on the Dorset and Somerset line, which coupled with the use of Thomas Tredgold as surveying engineer would have produced a very modern railway for the period.

The 1826 map of Somerset and Dorset shows over 100 miles of proposed railways, with parliamentary sanction for 49 miles, and about 6 miles of railway already in use, but not one line to London in sight. This gives an idea of the importance still given to coastal shipping in the 1820s, with railways just considered as a means of transporting goods to the nearest port rather than arms in a future national network. Eventually much of the proposed route of the Dorset & Somer-

Right - The Middlebere Plateway wagons were more technically advanced than their Welsh counterparts and only required two small horses to shift 10 tons of ball clay 3½ miles to Middlebere Quay.

Bottom - The 1870s built Lewin engine, 'Tiny', at Goathorn Pier c1907. Richard E Pinney is aboard the wagon and S J Stiff is stood alongside. Mr Pinney was Manager in the 1880/1890 period and was succeeded by Mr Stiff.

Ben Buxton collection

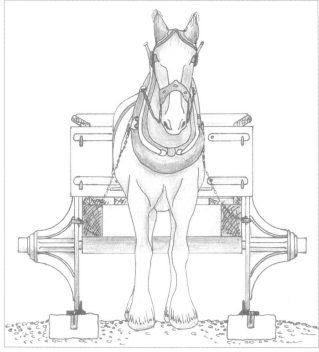

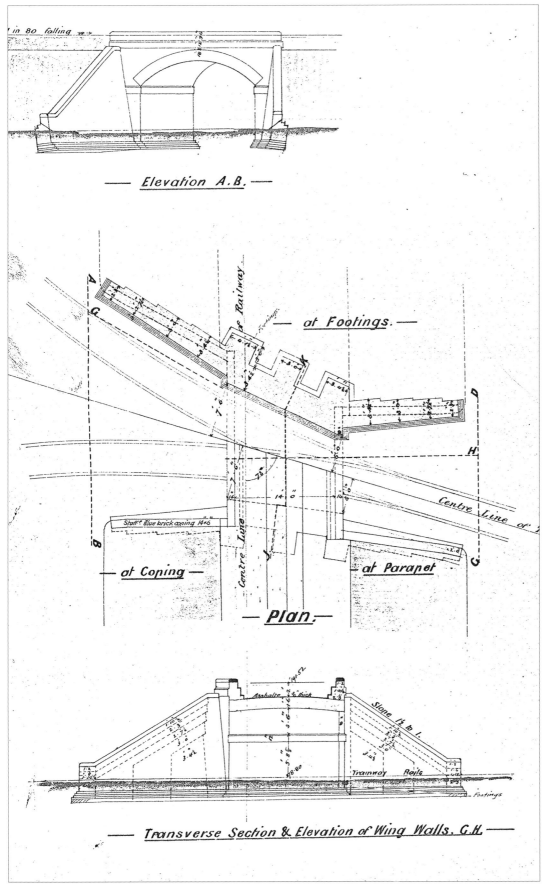

— Elevation A.B. —

— at Footings. —

— Plan. —

— at Coping —

— at Parapet —

— Transverse Section & Elevation of Wing Walls. G.H. —

set Canal and Railway, became the route of the Somerset and Dorset Railway, whilst the southern end of the line became the Wareham to Hamworthy section of the Southampton and Dorchester Railway.

Poole Harbour

The fortunes of the port of Poole played an important part in the formation of the rail system in Dorset and were partly determined by the actions of Napoleon's forces.

For some years, Poole Harbour had been host to transatlantic trade with Newfoundland, this prior to the outbreak of hostilities with France. But with Europe engulfed in war and thus unable to trade with America, it created a bonanza for the British transatlantic trade through Poole.

When peace returned in 1815 and with it the re-opening up of European ports to transatlantic trade, Poole began to suffer. By the 1820s the number of transatlantic ships using Poole was beginning to fall and the merchants looked to coastal trading to fill the gap. Clay export was one such trade, encouraged by the building of several transshipment sheds on Hamworthy Quay during the 18th and 19th centuries, all at the Poole council's own expense. These were leased to B. Fayle & Co. in 1813, Pike Bros. until 1825, and Thomas Wanhill from 1845. Channel Islands and French trade was also encouraged, which despite many and various setbacks over the years, has also provided the Hamworthy branch with much goods traffic over the past

150 years. The resurgence of the Dorset and Somerset Canal and Railway in 1825 was another attempt to provide the port with coal traffic from Somerset, manufactured goods from Yeovil, and agricultural produce from the rural areas of mid Dorset and Somerset.

Further west, during the 1840s Weymouth was beginning to rival Poole as a port and much political manoeuvering was done to ensure any railway proposal did not favour Weymouth over Poole as a route to London. One such meeting was held at Weymouth in October 1844, attended by deputations from Southampton, Poole , Wareham, Weymouth, Bridport, the Southampton & Dorchester Rly. and the GWR, including its Chairman, Charles Russell and Engineer Isambard Kingdom Brunel.

Mr.Castleman defended the Southampton & Dorchester proposal by stating that the route had been inspected by the Duke of Wellington and he had expressed his approval on account of its near approach to the coast: thus it greatly facilitated the defence of the country. With such formidable support the meeting found in favour of the Southampton & Dorchester, allied to the Wilts Somerset & Weymouth from Dorchester to Weymouth. (Even so both lines would be existence for some before a physical connection was provided between the two.)

In February 1847 the Poole Borough Council petitioned the House of Commons to block the Wilts Somerset and Weymouth Railway's proposal for a branch to Blandford, in favour of an LSWR backed scheme from Wimborne to Bruton via Templecombe and Blandford. This would have formed a junction with the Salisbury and Yeovil extension of the LSWR line.

In addition to the existing main line railways, the Bristol and English Channel Junction Railway was being promoted by Poole merchants and landowners, to provide a direct route from the Port of Poole to Bristol. Unfortunately they did not succeed, and today there is still no direct trunk road or rail link between Poole and Bristol.

With the arrival of the railway in Poole, the population started to grow, and the first commercialised pottery moved into the area. This was shortly followed by many others, largely manufacturing bricks, pipes, chimney pots, tiles and ornamental stoneware. The railways improved the supply of coal needed to fire the kilns in the area, and in many cases provided transport for the finished goods outwards. Items such as drainage pipes and chimney pots were packed with locally grown gorse to prevent breakage during transit.

As Bournemouth started to grow in size during the 1850s, the railways and the potteries flourished, supplying the people and materials to build the town. Subsequently, the period following the Second World War saw a gradual decline in the potteries and brickworks, until all but three had closed by the 1970s. Poole and Purbeck potteries continued making their distinctive tableware, and Carters Tiles were still producing wall and floor tiles (Carters supplied the tiles for toilets during the rebuilding of Waterloo station). Poole Pottery can be seen in the background of many B4 photographs taken on Poole Quay and a display cabinet of their wares was a feature of Poole station booking hall during the 1970s. A recent asset-striping exercise robbed Poole Pottery of its Quayside factory site, and left the company bankrupt just before Christmas 2006. Thankfully a rescue attempt has allowed Poole Pottery to continue in production, albeit on a much smaller scale.

This page and opposite -

Bridge 13 where the Plateway passed under the Swanage Branch

TO BE CONTINUED

THE LBSCR C2 and C2X GOODS ENGINES

Gerry Bixley

(Continued from Issue 9)

Table 3: C2X Locos Variations					
A	**B**	**C**	**D**	**E**	**F**
Rebuilt with all alterations; Re-boilered, new spring hangers, altered brakes, extended guard-irons. (1)	**As 'A' and subsequently fitted with double-dome boiler. (2)**	**Rebuilt, retaining original spring hangers, but with altered brakes and extended guard-irons. (3)**	**As 'C' and subsequently fitted with double-dome boiler. (4)**	**Rebuilt -but re-boilered only.**	**As 'E' and known to have subsequently carried double-dome boiler. (5)**
434	434	440	440	438	438
437	444	441	441	442	451
444	447	446	446	443	523
445	450	448	448	451	524
447	522	449	543	521	526
450	525	543		523	527
522	528	546		524	535
525	532			526	537
528	534			527	539
532	538			529	540
534	541			535	548
538	544			536	549
541	545			537	552
544	550			539	
545	551			540	
547	553			548	
550	554			549	
551				552	
553					
554					

Note 1: This applied to all engines up to September 1911. the last dealt with Nos. 437 and 528.
Note 2: Only Nos. 437, 445 and 547 appear not to have a double-dome boiler.
Note 3: Nos 446, 448 and 543 had brakes and guard-irons altered in later years.
Note 4: Only Nos 449 and 546 appear not to have had double-dome boilers.
Note 5: Only Nos. 442,443,521,529 and 536 appear not to have had double-dome boilers.

Opposite - *Detail of cab / tender on No. 32525.*

Alan Blackburn

THE LBSCR C2 and C2X GOODS ENGINES

No.	Date Rebuilt	Brakes Modified	Spring Hangers Modified	Guard irons Extended	Double-Dome Boiler Carried	Tender Change	Loco Condemned
					Table 4: C2X Locos Summary		
521	1/1925	No	No	No	No	C3	12/1961
522	9/1910	Yes	Yes	Yes	5/1934 - 5/1938	LSW	10/1961
523	4/1924	No	No	No	10/1935 - 4/1939, 6/1944 - 1/1949, 5/1954 - 4/1959	LSW	2/1962
524	10/1912	No	No	No	3/1933 - 11/1941		3/1958
525	12/1910	Yes	Yes	Yes	1/1937 - 1/1942		1/1962
526	6/1940	No	No	No	6/1940 - 3/1945, 10/1949 - 12/1955		2/1960
527	10/1939	No	No	No	10/1939 - 9/1943, 7/1955 - 11/1960		11/1960
528	9/1911	Yes	Yes	Yes	7/1931– 8/1936	C3 / LSW	2/1961
529	4/1924	No	No	No	No		9/1959
532	7/1911	Yes	Yes	Yes	4/1948 - 4/1954	LSW	5/1960
534	5/1911	Yes	Yes	Yes	2/1921 - 9/1927, 1/1942 - 6/1949		9/1961
535	12/1939	No	No	No	12/1939 - 12/1943, 1/1948 - 2/1962		2/1962
536	6/1924	No	No	No	No		3/1961
537	8/1924	No	No.	No	Believed 10/1929 - 10/1932		4/1957
538	4/1910	Yes	Yes	Yes	2/1933 - 9/1935, 3/1947 - 10/1953		12/1961
539	6/1924	No	No	No	Believed 11/27 - 4/1931, 10/1943 - 2/1951	LSW	11/1961
540	12/1922	No	No	No	7/1941 - 12/1946		4/1958
541	5/1910	Yes	Yes	Yes	Believed 4/1926 - 4/1928, 10/1959 - 1/1961		1/1961
543	10/1915	Yes	No	Yes	9/1925 - 10/1928, 4/1956 - 10/1960		10/1960
544	1/1911	Yes	Yes	Yes	Believed 6/1929 - 5/1940		11/1961
545	7/1908	Yes	Yes	Yes	3/1921 - 7/1935, 5/1956 - 12/1961	C3	12/1961
546	6/1912	Yes	No	Yes	No	C3	4/1961
547	10/1908	Yes	Yes	Yes	No	C3 / LSW	11/1961
548	3/1925	No	No	No	11/1937 - 5/1941, 10/1955 - 11/1961		11/1961
549	10/1912	No	No	No	11/1941 - 9/1947 - 2/1950 - 8/1955		12/1961
550	11/1910	Yes	Yes	Yes	3/1927 - 4/1932, 7/1944 - 12/1948, 10/1950 - 6/1956		12/1961
551	2/1909	Yes	Yes	Yes	3/1921 - 1/1926, 5/1955 - 2/1960		2/1960
552	1/1940	No	No	No	4/1944 - 3/1950	LSW	6/1961
553	10/1908	Yes	Yes	Yes	1/1921 - 7/1926, 3/1951 - 10/1955		8/1961
554	4/1911	Yes	Yes	Yes	7/1921 - circa 1930, 4/1933 - 1/1936		2/1960

Opposite top - *C2X as BR No. 32545. early BR livery, only the boiler and injectors show Ashford's influence. J H Aston*

Opposite bottom - *C2X as No. 32446 at Norwood Junction, 7 May 1956, with C3 tender. L G Marshall / G Bixley collection.*

Opposite top - C2X No. 32541 at Horsham 10 May 1959. Typical late condition with second BR crest.
J Scrace

Opposite bottom - C2X No. 32528. A newly rebuilt LBSC / LSW hybrid tender appears to have been attached.
Photomatic / G Bixley collection.

This page, top - C2X No. 32523 at Horsham, 24 August 1959. LBSC / LSW tender can be clearly seen.
J Scrace

This page, bottom - C2X No. 32525, tender top.
A Blackburn

No.	Double-Dome Boiler Carried	No.	Double-Dome Boiler Carried
Table 5: C2X Boiler Detail			
434, B434, 2434, 32434	3/1921 - 1/1927, 1/1938 - 6/1941, 8/1949 - 10/1954	534, B534, 2534	2/1921 - 9/1927, 1/1942 - 6/1949
2438, 32438	7/1938 - 6/1947, 6/1953 - 12/1958	2535, 32535	12/1939 - 12/1943, 1/1948 - 2/1962
32440	9/1952 - 10/1958	B537, 2537	Believed 10/1929 - 10/1932
B441	7/1927 - 7/1929	2538, 32538	2/1933 - 9/1935, 3/1947 - 19/53
2444, 32444	8/1940 - 6/1945, 3/1957 - 3/1960	B539, 2539, 32539	Believed 11/1927 - 4/1931, 10/1943 - 2/1951
2446, 32446	7/1945 - 5/1949	2540	7/1941 - 12/1946
B447, 2447	6/1928 - 4/1934	B541, 32541	Believed 4/1926 - 4/1928, 4/1956 - 10/1960
2448	11/1933 - 5/1942	B543, 32543	9/1925 - 10/1928, 4/1956 - 10/1960
B450, 2450, 32450	11/1926 - 1/1931, 6/1944 - 8/1950	B544, 2544	Believed 6/1929 - 5/1940
B451, 2451, 32451	1/1928 - 1/1931, 2/1939 - 2/1944, 3/1950—8/1952	545, B545, 2545, S2545, 32545	3/1921 - 7/1935, 5/1956 - 12/1961
2522	5/1934 - 5/1938	2548, 32548	11/1937 - 5/1941, 10/1955 - 11/1961
2523, 32523	10/1935 - 4/1939, 6/1944 - 1/1949, 5/1954 - 5/1959	2549, 32549	11/1941 - 9/1947, 2/1950 - 8/1955
2524	3/1933 - 11/1941	B550, 2550, 32550	3/1927 - 4/1932, 7/1944 - 12/1948, 10/1950 - 6/1956
2525	1/1937 - 1/1942	551, B551, 32551	3/1921 - 1/1926, 5/1955 - 2/1960
2526, 32526	6/1940 - 3/1945, 10/1949 - 12/1955	2552, 32552	4/1944 - 3/1950
2527, 32527	10/1939 - 9/1943, 7/1955 - 11/1960	553, B553, 32553	1/1921 - 7/1926, 3/1951 - 10/1955
2528	7/1931 - 8/1936	554, B554, 2554	7/1921 - Circa 1930, 4/1933 - 1/1936
S2532, 32532	4/1948 - 4/1954		

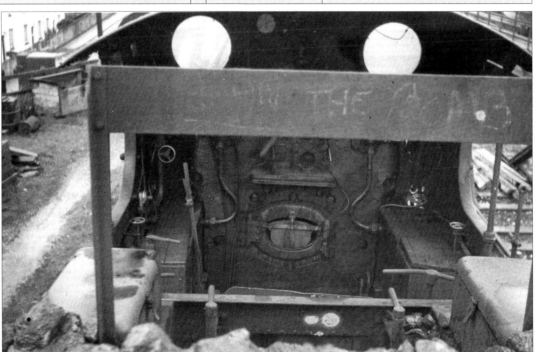

Opposite and this page -

Detail of C2X No. 32525.
All A Blackburn

Opposite top - C2X as SR No. 2550 at Horsham derailed in wartime condition showing tender detail.

G Bixley collection.

Opposite bottom - C2X No. 32543 at Horsham derailed 30 May 1957.

J Scrace

Above - No. 32543, Horsham, 30 May 1957.

J Scrace

Right - C2X No. 32521 at Horsham 18 April 1953. Driver Scrace and Fireman Manville.

J Scrace

Above - C2X No. No. 32527 at Southwater, 14 March 1959. 9.02 am freight from Hove to Three Bridges.   J Scrace.
Bottom - C2X No. No. 32527 at Christ's Hospital 28 February 1959 with 9.02 freight from Hove to Three Bridges.   J Scrace

'REBUILDING'-THE LETTERS AND COMMENTS PAGE(S)

As ever, it is a pleasure to record some of the contributions and comments received recently. In no particular order then we start with a note from John Davenport.

"Apologies for reappearing, but you shouldn't put so much in that jogs my dormant memories, even if you should be the result. SW9 and the Waterloo and City. I travelled on the original stock once - from Bank - I was seven and terrified. I use the line a lot from 1954 onwards. The bit about leaving the platform at bank was roughly correct. A sensible improvement in the tunnel or slopes, was the provision of a railed-off passage wide enough to take the contra-flow passengers. If you were in the back of a rush-hour train, you would normally just about reach the bottom of the slope as the next train could be heard approaching.

"Some bright spark had the idea that a bit of extra crowd control was needed. So one Monday morning the City workers were confronted by a chicane of steel post barriers across the bottom of the step. The result, reached very quickly, was that the whole thing gummed up solid. I wasn't a very early traveller, but when I arrived at Bank after some delays and the train doors were opened, you couldn't get out because both platforms were full! I think some people went back to Waterloo as the safest option.

"Fortunately someone saw the potential for a major disaster in the evening rush-hour, and the barriers disappeared. These were in the days before the Travelator."

John also forwarded a note some months back which should have appeared in Issue 9. It is one to make us all chuckle and concerns the delays consequent upon the collapse of Clapham Junction 'A' box. "I caught my usual train to work, which originated as the 6.45 am from Salisbury. We made normal progress until about New Malden, after which we didn't make much. Fortunately I, and my two travelling companions, had seats.

"Somewhere after Raynes Park we really stuck, opposite a house with a very charming lady who put on a great show for her captive audience!

"Back to trains. Eventually we reached Wimbledon, where we were turfed out, and found out why. I think it was after 10.30 am. As it was Monday, I think we had a 'Merchant' and the crew were off the footplate and at the water column like rabbits. One bonus was that we didn't have to pay for our onward travel over the District."

Next some words from Alastair Wilson, "I have just been transcribing some memoirs of my father who commuted from Etchingham to Charing Cross in the years 1947-1950. (He was working in the War Office). He remarked "The 8.1 from Etchingham was a popular train with business men & sported a first class "club" car. This had upholstered swivel arm chairs & you could order coffee or gin & tonic or any other drink you liked". I knew that a number of the trains on the Charing Cross-Hastings line had a third-class Pullman in their make-up – at that time, the 10.38 up from Robertsbridge and the 12.25 from Charing Cross were two – but I never knew of a first-class saloon in any train formation (not that I ever trav-elled first-class when I was a boy!). I'm sure one of our readers can give me chapter and verse for such a vehicle?" - *any suggestions please?*

Now one, the sender of which had better remain anonymous, "The Dorchester article is fascinating. I used to run around our Woking garden with a circular sticker on my forehead pretending to be the *Cunarder*...... I don't find running such an attraction, these days."

By e-mail we received some interesting feedback from Phillip Childs on Martin Dean's recent piece piece on 'The Southern and the Silver Screen.' "If you get a chance to see the 1941 Arthur Askey Gainsborough film 'The Ghost Train', the opening titles appear against the rolling back drop of the South Western mainline between Fleet and Winchfield, finishing at Hook. It seems that the filming was done from the rear carriage of a train on the up fast and the film is run backwards. We are treated to the wonderful sight of all those LSWR lower quadrant pneumatic signals into the bargain!, and speaking of which I would love to see an article on this system sometime. *(- so would we.)*

"Moving on, living in the Frimley area I couldn't believe my eyes when watching the Will Hay film "Goose steps out", in the part where our gallant knight, Will, pinches a German plane and makes landfall somewhere in the UK: with the plane now out of control you see it heading along a railway line. I've identified it from the brief clip, again of the South Western mainline this time passing the Kings Head pub just as you come out of the cutting at Deepcut. You can just make out the lines dropping down to the Frimley line to Ash Vale and the rising ground on the left is where Farnborough Abbey looks down. There are some other Southern shots in this film, possibly of the same junction but I am not sure, also one of a 'Lord Nelson' charging towards the camera.

"And finally as the two Ronnies would say, take a look at "Waterloo Road", staring John Mills and Stewart Granger, some lovely shots taken round the terminus in late Southern days. Hope this is interesting for you." - *it certainly is, thank you.* "P.S. just remembered having a look in the SR subterranean control centre with its blast wall and gas proof door adjacent to Oriental Road in Woking, close to where the trains shunt to east end carriage sidings , there wasn't much left in there but like many I had no idea of its existence until recent years." *(The wartime Woking Control Office is referred to in the piece on Deepdene, in the new 'Southern War Wartime Special Part 2 - Ed.)*

Now from Tom Dethridge, who apologises for typing errors in his note - please, it is me who should apologise for the ones that slip through at this end. Tom commences with some kind words, appreciated indeed, and continues with various pertinent observations, "In No. 6, the headcode on the goods headed by the rebuilt H15 (not 336, probably 330) on page 63 would indicate between Salisbury-Eastleigh or Eastleigh-Fratton. Next is not specifically a railway one, but I know many rail observers also find interest in other forms of transport. Some readers may have been surprised that in the view by the Meon Valley line, p.46-47 Issue 6), all the Army Vehicles including the tanks, carry civilian registration numbers: all registered in the Middlesex series. This in fact applied to all three services up to WWII. At a later date, the services were accorded exclusive lettering and / or numbers in the format DD LL DD (D = digits, L = letters).

"Turning to No. 7 and Mr Duffell's picture of a BEL unit on royal duty at Liphook. There were four or five occasions when such workings occurred on the Portsmouth Direct in the 1950s, including: 20 July 1951 - Princess Elizabeth, Waterloo - Portsmouth & Southsea to open the Nuffield Servicemen's Club: Headcode 07, 15 June 1953 - Queen and Duke, Windsor - Portsmouth Harbour for Coronation Fleet Review: Headcode 04, return the next day. It was also reported that the

BEL unit conveyed the Queen Mother between Waterloo and Portsmouth on the same day. I find this questionable, using one unit on two different workings on the same day. But it was also reported that Princess Margaret and other royals were conveyed to Portsmouth on 15th in a 6-PUL unit (not identified). Or is it possible that a second different BEL unit was used. Perhaps someone may know?

"14 October 1954 - Duke of Gloucester, Victoria - Portsmouth Harbour to welcome the Emperor of Ethiopia on his arrival for a state visit; the BEL returned to London with guests, headcode double blank. The Emperor and the Duke travelled to London in a Pullman train hauled by BB pacific No 34088.

"The only one of the above that Mr Duffell's photo fits

A slight puzzler - any information would be useful. 'U' class No. 31806 is seen north of Winchester - Wallers Ash tunnel is in the background, with what may well be a Portsmouth working. 1 August 1958.   Tony Molyneaux

is the first, (July 1951) working. It was unit No 3052 that carried out all the above and this seems to have been the set of choice for special duties - did 3052 have some special fitting or facility which led to this choice?

"On another topic, Mr Eltham's LSWR photos of the 1920s were of great interest, in particular that of the ROD 2-8-0 on the up Southampton line goods and I for one should be delighted to see more. *(Not sure there are any, we will enquire - Ed).*

"The article on the SR in films recalls the absolute joy of Will Hay & Co in "Oh! Mr. Porter" - my local Odean in Cosham had its gala opening with this film, attended by Mr. Hay. You mention that Adams 'Flyer' No. 657 and goods No. 3509 were fitted with shortened chimneys for the film; these reportedly were borrowed from a Brighton 'B4' or '13' engines and at one time I had a picture of this change. I thought it improved the appearance, others considered it sacrilege!" *(If the photo still exists we would love to borrow it to include - Ed.)*

Vivian Orchard passed a note, with some more wonderful images, *(- they are 'in the can' ready for use soon),* and with a comment over the new Waterloo & City stock. " Some of the new stock I remember seeing in Effingham Junction car sheds before introduction."

Another item, long overdue for inclusion comes from Alan Morris. "In Issue 2 there is a photograph of a Scammel somewhere in Watford. My wife was born in Watford, and on looking at the picture, reckons it could have been taken near the Hollywell Isolation Hospital. This was less than half a mile from the Scammel factory. My wife has memories of watching lorries leaving the factory with new Scammels on their backs.

"Now for a request, as a driver on the railway, I was briefly based at Charing Cross and have an interest in the various EMUs used on the Southern. I know steam will always be the first priority but I hope future articles will cover electric units." *(We would dearly love to feature more on EMUs, their workings, make up etc etc. I hope material to feature this will be available in the future, after all it is all part of the Southern scene - Ed.)*

Our regular friend and contributor, Eric Best, passes some inside knowledge on various of the illustrations in Issue 7. "Page 55. The photo of 32421 is very interesting as it shows the boiler used for supplying hot water for the bosh and workshop troughs at the top of No. 2 bay in the Erecting Shop. Between the boiler and the wall was the heat exchanger that was worked on during bank holidays. This was mainly descaling the tubes. The boiler was fed by an injector LH side and a Weir pump on the RH side.

"The grounded guards van body was used by the engine testing crews whose home base was Eastleigh Loco. The photo was taken from the top of the wood shed used for steam testing locos ex-works. The wood for this was old wagon sides (which was Pitch Pine very straight grain).

"The loco that worked the RAEs establishment site was a Hawthorne Leslie 0-4-0ST, No. 3135/15. This loco came to Eastleigh for repair. It was parked at the top of No. 4 bay.

However, the story I heard was that it would cost too much so it was never done and just went away again. It still survives though, as No. 37 on the IOW.)

Much other correspondence has been received, amongst others from M G Harvey and Ivan Jenkins on the topic of the Signalling School at Clapham Junction. Rather than précis this in this issue, there is sufficient, with more illustrations, for a further item on the subject which it is planned to include in Issue. 11.

With many thanks also to Mike Little, Tony Logan Roger Macdonald, Eric Penn and Eric Youldon.

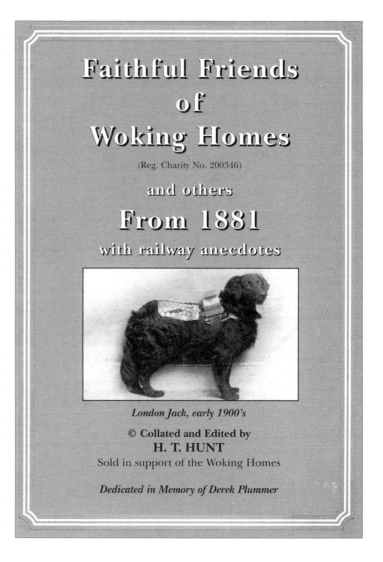

Faithful Friends of Woking Homes

(Reg. Charity No. 200346)

and others

From 1881

with railway anecdotes

London Jack, early 1900's

© Collated and Edited by
H. T. HUNT
Sold in support of the Woking Homes

Dedicated in Memory of Derek Plummer

We don't normally do reviews, but this is all for a valiant cause. If anyone is interested in more information on 'Woking Homes' and in particular the part played by the various collecting dogs, this little booklet makes a fascinating addition to the bookshelf. 'A5' size, 56 pages and £3.50 also make it reasonably priced.

Available from Woking Homes.

Bland and almost feature-less this is the main line station at Porton looking east towards Salisbury. Opened in 1857 it was extended in the form seen from 1899 onwards and reached its peak during the First World War when the narrow gauge line had interchange with the goods yard sidings situated on the north side of the line. Porton 'box dated from late 1870 and was supplied to house the levers that had previously stood in the open. The frame was a Stevens 13 lever example.

Seen in the opposite direction circa 1912 viewed towards Grateley and Basingstoke. There was much similarity with the layout here and that at Oakley, east of Porton (- the former station featured in 'Southern Way No 8'). Compared with the view opposite, there is little in the way of major visual change that occurred over almost 60 years, one of the most noticeable item being the way the cutting side opposite the approaching train has been completely taken over with vegetation in the right hand view.   *The Lens of Sutton Collection*

POISONOUS PORTON

The village of Porton lies in the valley of the River Bourne a few miles to the east of Salisbury and is surrounded by Porton Down, and to today's generation the name will be fairly meaningless. To those of slightly more mature years the name conjures up a more sinister memory. For in 1948 Porton Down became the Microbiological Research Department and the next two decades aimed at providing Britain with the means to arm itself with a modern nerve-agent-based capability and to develop specific means of defence against these agents. However, back in the 19th century this seemed light years in the future.

The South Western Basingstoke & Salisbury Extension Act was authorised in August 1846 and allowed for construction of a direct line between the two towns via Andover. The cost was estimated at £700,000 for the 35 mile route, and three years was allowed for construction. Building commenced in July 1847 with Thomas Brassey appointed as main contractor. With the depression following on from the earlier Railway Mania the company found the raising of capital difficult. By October 1848 the money had run out and the work lay abandoned, waiting for better times. The construction time authorised by the original Act expired, extension of time was requested from Parliament. This was granted in 1848 and again in 1850. In 1851 a meeting of landowners took place in Andover and decided to promote the Basingstoke & Salisbury company to take over the derelict South Western works. The London & South Western (Basingstoke & Salisbury) Act was passed in August 1853 Brassey and his navvies returned to the abandoned works. The line was opened from Basingstoke to Andover in July 1854.

In 1855 the South Western Consolidation Act authorised the westward extension to Salisbury. With Brassey still the main contractor the line was opened to Salisbury (Milford) on 1 May 1857. Having reached Salisbury we can return to Porton to take a closer look at the station and its associated light railway.

The station was constructed on the hillside between overbridge No 210 and underbridge No 211, and was originally a small wayside station on a single line with passing loop. The section to Salisbury (Tunnel Junction) was doubled in June 1868; that eastwards to Grateley followed in July 1870. The following September approval was sought for the construction of a signal cabin which was to house 13 levers and associated signalling equipment.

In the early 1890s the War Office purchased much land on Salisbury Plain and extensive military manoeuvres were programmed to be carried out in 1898. However, although Porton station was nearest to the action it missed out due to the short platforms and small goods yard. This was amended in 1899 with the authorisation to construct longer platforms, with an enlarged goods yard laid to the north of the line.

Various improvements followed, with the installation in 1902 of a steel girder footbridge (No 210A); before this passengers had to use a barrow crossing opposite the signalbox.

The main station buildings were situated on the up side. The two storey station house, built in 1857, incorporated the stationmaster's accommodation with public access through

A 1960 view, again seen eastwards. The effects of weather have taken their toll on the western end of the station building, likewise the lean-to on the same end of the main building which has now been rendered. To pass a few moments, it is perhaps interesting to try and spot the differences that have taken place over the years - we found 12, not including those mentioned above, without too much difficulty.........(the list is on page 47.) In the distance under the footbridge (No 210A) the stone bridge (No 210) was that used by the Porton Military Railway.
The Lens of Sutton Collection

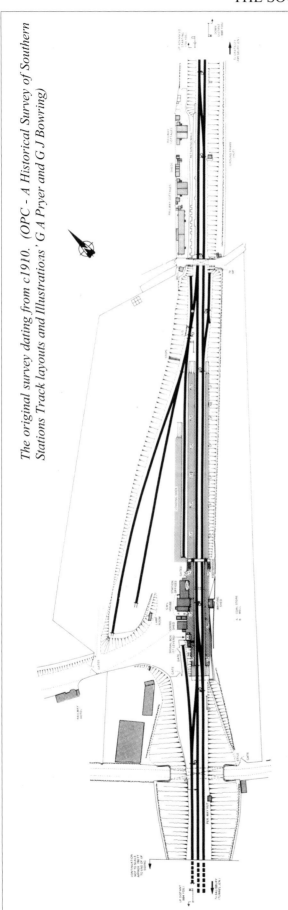

The original survey dating from c1910. (OPC - A Historical Survey of Southern Stations Track layouts and Illustrations' G A Pryer and G J Bowring)

a door into the booking hall and then on to the platform, the only undercover area being under part of the roof of single section. Toilets and a waiting room completed the passenger accommodation. Moving along the platform there were a coal store and a signalbox with adjacent pump house that supplied the station's water supply. The porter drew the short straw in being responsible for supplying water as required. Completing the facilities was a goods shed with access by a sliding door from the platform. Opposite the station building, on the down platform, a wooden waiting shelter sufficed.

For many years the station was lit by oil lamps. However towards the end these were replaced by Tilley lamps.

Just to the east of bridge No 210 three pairs of railway cottages were constructed, together with some sheds. These, like the station, drew their water supply from wells.

As already mentioned the goods yard was expanded to cope with the military traffic. Behind the Up platform was a long siding which also served the cattle pen. Between 1917 and 1953 the two other sidings were flanked by the lines of the narrow gauge sidings of the Porton Camp line. There was also a 2-ton crane, later supplemented by the Army's 3-ton steam crane, and vehicle dock. Both were useful for the transfer of items to the nearby army camp. A long Up refuge siding was supplied which could accommodate a locomotive and 40 wagons.

With the increase in private vehicle ownership and the transfer of freight from rail to road the station's end was inevitable. The goods yard closed on 10 September 1962. The station survived for a further six years, closing on 9 September 1968, four months after the signalbox's demise.

The Basingstoke and Salisbury line itself escaped the worst of Beeching's excesses and, although several stations, goods yards and associated branches were no longer considered viable, it survives into the modern age together with bridge No 210 which gives access to a storage site to the south of the line. Nurtured by the Southern Region and Network SouthEast, the line now prospers with long-distance commuting to London. The 1990s saw a complete route modernisation, new trains, a new depot at Salisbury and station improvements.

Porton Light Railway

In 1916 the War Office acquired much of the nearby Idmiston Down for what was to become the Royal Engineers Experimental Station, Porton, the intention being to develop defences against chemical warfare. World War 1 was at its height at this time and the use of poison gas was commonplace on the European battlefields. In 1917 the Army decided that it had to improve access to the camp, which by now accommodated over 1,000 men and extensive facilities.

The 60 cm line (sometimes seemingly erroneously referred to a 2 feet), commenced in the goods yard between the sidings and swung round to the north of the site in order to gain height to cross the main line by bridge No 210. The bridge, built as an accommodation crossing had to be substantially reinforced.

Virtually all the construction materials arrived in Porton's goods yard, starting with the wood for the trestles, sleepers, rails and fastenings together with the ballast requirements. Once the locomotives and wagons were on site, deliveries could be transferred to the narrow gauge and sent to the various camps that were constructed. Passengers were also carried between Porton and the camps. The greatest number was 18,663 in December 1918 along with 1,434 tons of freight. With traffic at these

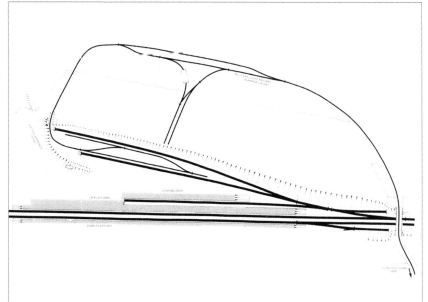

Top - *This plan dates from c1916 and shows the layout of the goods yard after construction of the Porton Military Railway. The exchange sidings are clearly shown along with ample storage space as the narrow gauge line circles the boundary to gain height. (OPC - A Historical Survey of Southern Stations Track layouts and Illustrations' G A Pryer and G J Bowring)*

Bottom - *The 3 ton steam crane installed at Porton LSWR probably at the time the narrow gauge railway was built. It is seen here in November 1917. Used no doubt for general freight as well, it was invaluable in the transfer of materials from standard to narrow gauge vehicles. K P Norris, in his work on the Porton Military Railway for the Bourne Valley Historical, record and Conservation Society, records as follows, "Work started at Porton on 7 March 1916 when a Sergeant Major Dobbs RE reported to Porton for permanent duty. On 13 March a gang of men from Messrs W E Chivers and Sons, Contractors of Devizes, started work on the circular trenches which were to dominate the Porton landscape for several decades. This gang was soon replaced by another under the control of the Officer in Charge of Works, who reported directly to the Commandant. On 30 March two Army huts arrived with instructions that one was to be used as an office and the second as a store (Carter, 1992). A letter which accompanied the instruction said, "These are all the huts which will be required." As it happened within two and a half years a camp had been built to house over 1000 men and major facilities had been built to enable experimental work to proceed. At the end of the Great War permanent buildings including married quarters were built and the establishment became known as Porton Camp to differentiate it from Porton village. The military presence remained until 1957. Since then the name Porton Camp has been replaced slowly by that of Porton Down. Today the name Porton Camp is used only by local people and by the Camp Recreation and Sports Club. The name can be seen on the lone sign post at the cross roads in Porton at Grid Reference SU 19093647. In 1917 access to the camp posed many difficulties. The only access was through the railway arch at Idmiston, now known as Idmiston Arch (Grid Reference SU 2017 3719). A decision was taken in 1917 to build a military railway of 24 inch gauge from Porton Station to Porton Camp. The materials and locomotives for the light railway came from H M Factory, Henbury which had closed in the autumn of 1916."*

A close up of the trestle during construction. This method avoided the need for the infill to raise the ground level to the required height. The four sappers are probably taking a break whist the photo was taken.

Courtesy BVHR&S

Near the camp was a small junction, referred to as the 'Y' junction, to allow track to be laid to facilities away from the main camp. At this point the track was at ground level.

Courtesy BVHR&S

The Winterbourne Trestle in the course of construction, necessary to bridge a dip south of the East Gomelton Road. When complete it ran for 600 feet at a maximum height of 16 feet. This extension of the Light Railway, on some plans referred to as a 'Tramway', diverged towards the 1917 Trench Mortar Experimental Station, located at the nearby village of Winterbourne Gunner - sometimes referred to as Porton South. This 2-mile rail link arrived later the original narrow gauge line and was not completed until sometime after November 1918. The maximum gradient was 1 in 40.

Entrance for the Light Railway to the magazine at Winterbourne Gunner - South Camp. Track was laid to major buildings, yet more magazines, the mortar positions, and the range itself.

Courtesy BVHR&S

The Porton station trestle as seen in November 1917. The cross roads in Porton village can be seen to the left of the picture.
Courtesy BVHR&S

levels thought was given to extending the standard gauge, but nothing came of the proposal.

By 1919 the line was operated by five steam locomotives, some 150 wagons and six passenger coaches. The locomotives were shedded at the camp and it was here that the workshops were. Passenger services ceased in 1937, when the Silver Star bus services, based inside the camp, replaced them.

The line was used to transport construction materials to building sites within the camp. These included the water tower which provided a head of water for the camp supply and the Headquarters building. One interesting story is a facility in which smoke flares were tested for the Royal Navy. This large concrete tank was known as HMS Porton; the sinking of which was announced by Lord Haw-Haw in 1942.

As Porton Camp expanded during the inter-war period and after World War 2 the railway was extended to serve much of the site. The last extensions appear to have been made in 1952 when a new Engineering Facility was built.

The railway continued in use until 1953/54 when the use of coal was discontinued in favour of oil although one reference mentions that coal was transferred to road haulage in the late 1940s when a Salisbury merchant gained the contract to supply the camp.

Locomotives

It seems that a total of five steam locomotives were in use at Porton on the narrow gauge line, four were 0-4-0STs with the other being an 0-6-0WT. Details are scarce and the following has been distilled from information published in the *Industrial Railway Record*.

Taking the latter first it was probably Hudswell Clarke W/No 1317 of 1918. By this date it would have been one of the 'standard' War Office steam locomotives of the type supplied to the forces to 'supply the trenches'. This one was however delivered direct to the War Office's Royal Engineers Experimental Station, Porton.

The first of the 0-4-0STs was DES (Department of Explosive Supplies) No 130, and appears to have been constructed by John Fowler in March 1898. Delivered new to the Llanelly Steel Co., it was with a dealer in 1916 so may well be the example seen at Porton.

The second singleton 0-4-0ST was Bagnall W/No 1674. New in 1901 to Swansea Corporation, it passed through a number of contracts before ending up with a dealer who rebuilt it to 2ft gauge and sold it to the Ministry of Munitions.

The remaining duo were of the Kerr Stuart 'Wren' type. W/Nos 2464 and 2465 were dispatched new in December 1915 to a contractor building a munitions factory at Dornoch. Both found their way south to W. E Chivers who was the contractor involved in the construction of the camp.

By the early 1920s the steam locomotives were on the market and motive power was supplied by internal combustion units. The Industrial Railway Society lists these as Baguley W/No 682 of 1917 and Motor Rail's W/Nos 1352 and 1353 of 1918. The latter two were WDLR locomotives Nos 3073 and 3074 that had seen service in France.

Also listed as being at Porton was a standard gauge 0-6-0T, Hawthorn Leslie W/No 3027 dating from 1913. Unless this was used in the goods yard at Porton it would have been of little use on a 2ft gauge line!

Top - *As with the main line the narrow gauge was ballasted. This was on the approach to Porton station and was probably for show as the sleepers appear to be well bedded in with earth.*

Bottom - *One of the Kerr Stuart 'Wrens' trailing a rake of 10 hoppers and pushing four flat wagons loaded with timber. By this date, January 1918, the trestle was complete.*   *Both courtesy BVHR&S*

This page, top - The bridge over the LSWR main line, No 210, seen here being strengthened to carry the additional weight of the railway and its trains.

This page, centre - Crossing the Downs with work in progress. The civilian workmen are being supervised by the sappers, complete with rudimentary levelling gear.

This page, bottom - Apart from the trestle at Porton station the main heavy engineering feature was the cutting at Porton Down. Note the steepness of the sides as the line was cut through chalk.

Opposite page, top - Constructing the revetment area for the armament storage magazine.

Opposite page, bottom - The lines were laid through a number of magazine buildings. This one containing 6in shells. I wonder what today's H&S officer would think!

All courtesy BVHR&S

Top - *The extension to the Trench Mortar Experimental Station involved the construction of Winterbourne trestle, seen here in the course of construction. 15)*

Bottom - *Extension of the railway for the foundations of what became Building 106. Both courtesy BVHR&S*

Top - The 6in Trench Howitzer site. The light railway runs to the front of the battery, with the LSWR main line on the embank,ment to the rear. ***Bottom*** - Four of the steam locomotives are seen in front of the locomotive shed in November 1917. The identities, as explained in the text are believed to be (L-R) Fowler 0-4-0ST, W/No 7227 of 1898, Bagnall 0-4-0ST W/No 1674 of 1901, Kerr Stuart 'Wren' 0-4-0STs W/Nos 2464 and 2465 of 1915. *Both courtesy BVHR&S*

Above - The camp water tower and lightly laid track alongside. This tank was the header for the water system to both the main camp and magazine. Materials for its construction were brought in by rail - having been offloaded at Porton (LSWR).
Right - Chronograph screen mounted on a flat truck. The mortar position, see also photograph on preceding page, was in line with the second - more distant screen.
                                                                      Both courtesy BVHR&S

Left - The original aim of the experimental work at Porton was to carry out trials in which chemical agents such as chlorine were released from cylinders. The trials were designed to measure how much of the gas found its way into trenches. Concentric circular trenches of 200 yards and 400 yards diameter were built and chemicals were released at the centre, so that no matter which way the wind blew the resultant cloud entered both the trench systems and its effects could be measured. On 17 March 1916, one hundred gas cylinders arrived from Oldbury, Birmingham but it was found almost impossible to cart them to the ground on account of the absence of proper roads - hence the railway.

Courtesy BVHR&S

'Wren' W/No 2465, as DES No 12. The 'home-built' cab was probably to keep out inclement weather whilst in use at Dornoch, where it was 'posted' prior to moving south to Porton. The cloth covering on the back of the cab was probably to save the driver's knuckles when applying the handbrake. The property seen on the right is one of the three pairs of railwaymen's cottages.

Courtesy BVHR&S

Readers wishing for more information are directed to the *Industrial Railway Record* No 148 for additional details.

Rolling Stock

There were over 150 items of rolling stock ranging from the large bogie wagons, capable of carrying some eight tons, down to the much smaller tipper trucks that were capable of being worked by the available manpower. Published sources state that six passenger-carrying vehicles were also in use, but no illustrations are known.

Probably due to the nature of the work at the site there are no recorded details of disposal. One can only assume that it was all scrapped on site by contractors.

References / further reading

Industrial Railway Record No 148, K. P. Norris, Industrial Railway Society
An Historical Survey of Selected Southern Stations, G. A. Pryer & G. J. Bowring, OPC/Ian Allan Publishing, 1980/20xx
Main Lines to the West: Part 1 — Basingstoke to Salisbury, John Nicholas & George Reeve, Irwell Press, 2008
Porton Military Railway, K. P. Norris, Bourne Valley Historical, Record & Conservation Society
Southern Main Lines — Basingstoke to Salisbury, Vic Mitchell & Keith Smith, Middleton Press, 1991

Special thanks are due to the Bourne Valley Historic Society, (Tony Goodenough - Archivist) for allowing access to material prepared by Keith Norris.

Just one example of the type of rolling stock uses at Porton. This is an 8-ton bogie wagon. The CWD standing for Chemical Warfare Department. One source states that the CWD stood for Canadian War Department which seems very unlikely. However World war 2 was to see a number of heavy freight 2-8-2 locomotives supplied to indian State Railways from Canada that were known by the ISR as the CWD class.

Courtesy BVHR&S

SPOT THE DIFFERENCE - *from pages 32 / 33*

Signal box nameboard
Finials on roof of main building
Lamp on footbridge
Smoke chutes on footbridge
Valance to signal box
Board crossing
Style of ground signal used for trailing crossover
Position and type of signs
Position of platform lamps
Poster boards on main building
Valance missing from end of downside waiting shelter
Number of barge boards on front of signal box.

WHO SAID - THE HORSE COMES BEFORE THE CART?

We have had these 'in stock' so to speak for some time, so it is certainly time they were used. Their origins are that kindly man from Lightmore Press, Ian Pope, who in conversation one day just happened to mention, "...are these any good for 'SW'?". Well who are we to refuse?

The builder is obvious; they did not just produce rolling stock, and clearly all were destined for Nine Elms, basic yet functional, driver comforts non-existent and yet typical of the period. One thing that did change in the following 40 years was that some weather protection was now provided - but for the load not the driver!

Terry Cole's Rolling Stock File No. 10
Postal Vehicles

Carrying mail was one of the functions of railways from the early days but information on services is often patchy. The Southern Railway originally had four main overnight mail trains: Waterloo – Bournemouth, Waterloo – Dorchester, Holborn Viaduct – Newhaven Harbour and London Bridge – Dover via Redhill of which the most important were the Dorchester and Dover services. Due to the requirements of the Royal Mail there were significant similarities between the postal vans of all companies. These vans fell into two types: Sorting Vans (BR classification POS) and Stowage Vans (sometimes called Postal Tenders) where unsorted bags of mail were stored (BR classification POT).

Opposite top - This is ex SECR Postal Stowage Van No 113 built in 1907 as one of five (Nos. 110 – 114) ordered to go with five Sorting Vans already constructed. It has a body length of 50ft 1in., is electrically lit and has a capacity of 9 tons. The five were renumbered as luggage vans 2018 -22 in 1923; however, 2018 -20 were reclassified back to postal vehicles in 1931 as Nos. 4954 – 6. No.113 (now 2021) was transferred to service stock in 1945, becoming 221.S. and allocated to Engineers Dept. Painting, London East Division. It is seen here at East Croydon on 10/3/48. Sister vehicles 4954/5/6 lasted on the Dover postal service until the end of the fifties.

Opposite bottom - This is former LSWR 44ft Postal Sorting Van No 13 seen here at Wimbledon as 1448 S on 21/4/48. Built in 1898 it had side gangways both ends, was gas lit, and was one of the vehicles used on the mail service to Dorchester. At some stage it was renumbered 5613 and then became SR number 4911 in the postal vehicle numbering block. A lavatory was added for staff in 1937 but the vehicle was withdrawn in 1939 on the arrival of the new Southern Railway vehicles. It was then used in the emergency control train at Wimbledon.

This page - The Southern built only eight post office vehicles: four sorting vans and four stowage vans. The four stowage vans Nos. 4957-60 were built in 1939 to Diagram 3196 with the standard Maunsell restriction 4 coach profile although with flat ends and offset gangways. One of these, S 4960, is seen here at Clapham Junction. on 14/5/52. Three vans were allocated to the Dorchester service and one to the London Bridge- Dover service. The Waterloo – Dorchester service was extended to Weymouth in 1960 and most of the
vehicles including 4960 continued on this service until replaced by converted BR stock in 1974. However there was still a requirement for them on the Dover run so they remained in traffic until 1976.
[All photos author's collection]

Confessions of a Steam Age Season Ticket Holder Part 2

extracts from a Waterloo commuters notebook

Keith Widdowson

(Continued from Issue 9)

Speed(y) merchants

There have been many articles detailing SR steam locomotive performances, the power ratio, output, coal usage in relation to speed, etc, over the years. I do not profess to know the ins and outs of why this happened or that occurred – all I remember (helped by extensive note taking at the time) is that it was a privilege to have witnessed and participated in the wonderful finale of Bulleid's Pacifics during the last few months of the Iron Horse's reign on the Waterloo services.

Several steam drivers adopted a "gung-ho" attitude and entered into the Indian summer scenario, obtaining previously unheard of speeds over the well-fettled permanent way formation theoretically provided for the new electrics. With most permanent way speed restrictions lifted, the newly re-laid track was an inevitable lure for certain drivers to push their machines to their limit.

Taking into consideration they were destined for the scrap yard in the not too distant future any failure/defect caused by excessive speed would be attributed to the hapless locomotive's poor run-down condition. Whilst some signalmen sometimes reported fast running (i.e. only possible by breaking the 85mph maximum steam was allowed) management seemingly turned a blind eye to such occasions preferring to promote the new clean image that the eventual inauguration of the brand-new electrics would provide (albeit three months later than originally anticipated!).

It was impossible to be aboard all the attempted 100mph runs but word of mouth usually ensured that most were known about - the drivers themselves "tipping" us off as regards which train/turn they were working. If, however, a poor performing Bulleid or any Standard 5MT was allocated to the designated train we looked elsewhere to chase our particular favourites or other "wants or needs". Whilst the acceleration and sound of them was sometimes spectacular the fastest speed I ever recorded with a Standard 5 was a mere 82mph. I was lucky enough eventually to obtain 30 instances of speeds over 90mph (see appendix) of which four attained the magic 100mph, with Merchant No. 35003 *Royal Mail* was perhaps the most prolific performer, certainly once Salisbury shed had "adopted" her, and she shook off her nickname "Royal Snail" with some unbelievable runs. Amongst the drivers perhaps Porter of Nine Elms could be guaranteed to obtain the most out of any given steed - he was not, however, immune from perform-

Merchant Navy No 35008 'Orient Line' ready for departure from Waterloo with the 15 30 to Weymouth on Wed 28th Sep 1966. I was to follow her for 630 miles over the next three days!

Having failed to restart the 17 09 Waterloo to Basingstoke from the normal stopping point adjacent to the signalbox WC No 34013 'Okehampton' had to reverse twice before obtaining "clean rail" – thus allowing me to obtain this shot during the 11 minutes delay collected. The date – 7ᵗʰ October 1964. www.southern-images.co.uk

ing more mundane duties having been seen shunting the bullion vans off of the 16.51 arrival on 21 September 1966 on an EDL! As regards the attempted ton speeds I can only assume the firemen who worked with such drivers were fully up to meeting the increased workload required – not for them was the need to visit any gym to induce Olympian muscles!

I will never forget the exhilarating feeling of anticipation, when crossing Battledown flyover, having stormed up Winchester bank, and attaining the through line at Worting Junction with signal sighting indicating a clear road, for possible high speeds ahead. The combination of an enthusiastic driver and a Bulleid in fine form was a heady mix which can never be recreated on today's PC railway system. The leading coach of these trains was not necessarily the best place for "normal" members of the public. With all available windows open and occupied by enthusiasts looking for mileposts in order to record speeds on our stopwatches and in our notebooks the inevitable coal dust, cinders and smoke poured in. Any attempt to concentrate sufficiently enough to read a paper or book surely must have been abandoned by the sometimes alarming hunting the coach took on at high speed! I do remember Optrex eye baths were frequently used by us upon reaching home in order to attempt to wash out grit trapped under the eyelids. Still to this day, even though I write right-handed, I wear my wristwatch on that arm because the left was always in use with a stop watch.

The two most travelled on trains

These were the 17.09 SX Waterloo to Basingstoke (102) and the 18.38 EWD Salisbury to Waterloo (109) occasions. Taking the 17.09 service first - the entry made in my notebook on 22 September 1964 reads as follows "This trip is the first of many – the idea being bump up my steam mileage

during the winter months – and to obtain a run behind every remaining Bulleid". Little did I realise that the seed for a nightly 'fix' of steam travel was sown - leading me to accumulate over 43,000 miles behind 91 (so far) of Bulleid's Pacifics. Firstly it was a weekly return visit to Woking, then twice weekly, then a double trip, i.e., returning for, and boarding, the 18.54 departure, then Basingstoke and eventually a nightly trip to Southampton. Throughout steam's reign I NEVER travelled in/out of Waterloo behind a diesel – sometimes having to travel on an EMU to Alton changing on to a DEMU 'over the Alps' in order to catch a returning steam service from Southampton to Waterloo. Obvious financial advantages were to be made, being a BR employee, by purchasing a privilege season ticket to Basingstoke – extended to Southampton for the princely sum of 10/- (50p) per week from March '66 to April '67. Returning to the 17.09 service - with other commuter services changing over to 'Warship' haulage or Class 33 and TC stock or Class 47 - this heavily loaded 10-coach commuter train remained, with a couple of isolated occasions in August '66, steam operated until just five weeks before the end – succumbing then to a Class 33. A schedule of 31 minutes for the non-stop 24½ miles to Woking was sometimes difficult to achieve because of the inner-suburban intensity of service, coupled with poor coal/condition of engine. Footplate rides were offered and gratefully accepted between Farnborough and Hook on several occasions with both Standard 5MT and 'West Country's being involved. The leading coach of the train was often a FO (First Open) and much to the annoyance of several bowler-hatted businessmen we used all to hang out of every available window to observe the signals and soak up the atmosphere of a steam engine working hard. Years later a senior manager at Waterloo said to me (myself having subsequently become a manager) that he recognised me from somewhere and hadn't we met before. Perplexed to begin with, when he mentioned that he lived at Farnborough

I realised, but feigned ignorance, that he was one of the many first class passengers who had frequently told us to "clear out of here"! During 1965 the 17.09 was rostered for a 70D 'West Country'. This engine was, at that time, off the 09.39 arrival that morning so I usually attempted to be around upon its arrival to plan that evening's activity. The fastest start to stop Waterloo to Woking I recorded was on 24 March 1966 with 'BoB' No. 34071. Passing Hampton Court Junction in 16m 22secs (WTT 18½) at 62mph (the maximum en route) we arrived Woking in 26m 21secs (WTT 31m). For one week in May 1967 light Pacific No. 34052 was allocated for the entire week and with Driver Evans(70A) in charge we had some spectacular accelerating starts out of Woking perhaps the best being on the Wednesday when, with 11 coaches, he took a mere 8m 33secs from Woking up to MP31 passing the "summit" at 70½ mph.

The second train – which became my most travelled on steam service - was the 18.38 from Salisbury to Waterloo. This sometimes "lightweight" train was worked by Basingstoke men to their home depot thence forward by a Nine Elms crew (having worked down on the 17.41 commuter train from Waterloo). Some phenomenal speeds were achieved between Basingstoke and Woking which have been well documented over the years in numerous publications. Salisbury turned out either whatever they didn't want or as dictated by the DMO Wimbledon office. TOPS reporting had yet to arrive on the scene but telephone contact was made every afternoon by Paul - whom I had always thought held the post of "power assistant" – who just happened to be a fellow enthusiast. Many years later I learnt that he should have only dealing with vans! When a known "keen" driver was rostered for the turn then the best mechanically "fit" steam engine was directed to work the train – Paul being 'guided' by us "puffer nutters". Every type of non-tank locomotive available was likely to be allocated: per-

haps the most surprising, from the occasions I was on board, was Patricroft-allocated Caprotti Standard 5MT No. 73133 on 18 November 1965 - having visited Eastleigh for attention. A creditable 27m 57secs from Woking to Waterloo with a maximum of 75mph at Hersham was achieved – even though thick fog was the predominant weather. The Salisbury train departed Basingstoke at 19.34 but was often early arriving there – on the up local. Arriving simultaneously on the up through was the 15.50 from Weymouth (departure 19.28) and instant decisions had to be made as to which locomotive was to be travelled with for those 47¾ miles to Waterloo. Those decisions were based on each individual's personal mileage with whatever turned up or if the Nine Elms driver on the Salisbury going for a high speed attempt. No longer will the familiar side rod clank of approaching Bulleids be heard - if only that the nightly decision was still available to us nowadays! As the end of steam approached and with the Weymouth going over to Class 73/TC - coupled with the preceding Channel Island Boat services not starting until high summer more time was spent in the nearby public house at Basingstoke. As an aside a similar scenario was enacted at Preston during 1967/8 whereby a receding number of steam trains meant a greater occupancy of alcoholic watering holes. Today's binge-drinking culture amongst teenagers can never use the 1955 Modernisation plans to eliminate the Iron Horse as their reason, can they!

On one occasion, after arrival at Waterloo, the guard remonstrated with the driver over the rough ride he had had in his brake – reminding him that there was (as was often the case) a 75mph restricted van within the formation! Having already showered the crew with congratulations (including a whip-round for the Southern Railway's Woking Orphanage) we remained very quiet and kept our stop-watches and notebooks well hidden!

Taking into account the locomotives not being in

An unusual visitor to Waterloo in the form of BR Class 4MT No 76012 on 28th January 1966 working the 15 38 parcels to Eastleigh. www.southern-images.co.uk

THE main man - Driver Porter thrashing up the bank leaving all others standing! Friday 21ˢᵗ April 1967 sees the Nine Elms driver riding up the approach road to Basingstoke shed.

Ascot – 'The Shakespearian Rail Tour' on 12ᵗʰ November 1966 at Ascot with WC No 34015 'Exmouth'. Driver Porter was to attain a seat-grabbing 75mph through Bracknell later!

prime condition it was a miracle that runs of such significance were happening at all *and* being recorded. A very creditable performance, for a Standard, was recorded on 14 June 1966, when No. 73171 working the 18.38 from Salisbury (load 5 coaches, 5 vans) and Driver Cummings (70A), with a maximum of a mere 74mph, attained even time from Basingstoke to Woking taking just 23m 22secs for the 23½ miles.

Dieselisation

Dealing firstly with the West of England services, which from September `64 were worked by 'Warships' (Class 42), but terminating at Exeter St Davids - there were many instances when 70E came to the rescue with whatever was available. Although they rarely worked west of Salisbury numerous instances were noted, such as, on the up services, Nos.

35029 (13 October 1964), 34052 (17 July 1965), 34063 (31 July 1965), and on 21 September 1966 No. 34052 on the 18.25 arrival from Exeter – she had been booked to work the 18 38 from Salisbury, and 34001 was substituted. As regards the down services I witnessed Nos. 34032 (05 June 1965), 34025 (18 November 1965), 34002 (31 May 1966), 34015(12 July 1966), 34093 (4 May 1967), 34089 (3 June 1967) with 34018 (16 June 1967) perhaps being the final substitution? From 28 November 1966 to 2 January 1967 the 19.00 from Waterloo was booked steam to Salisbury with the 'Warship' which had worked the 17.41 commuter train Waterloo to Salisbury working forward with the 19.00! On 06 December 1966, however, the 'Warship' ran out of fuel prior to working the 17.41 and No. 34019 stepped in! The following day the Warship failed on the inwards leg with No. 34019 coming to the rescue again!

The other dieselisation came in October 1966 when

'Lord Dowding' – my favorite Light Pacific. 23 journeys with her totaling 1,174 miles and by being allocated to 70E usually kept clean. I travelled with on her last passenger train – the 19 06 Basingstoke to Eastleigh(en route Bournemouth) on Friday 7th July 1967. This scene shows her after arriving at Basingstoke having worked the 17 09 from Waterloo with Driver Evans (70A) on 10/05/67 (she worked the 17 09 every day that week!).

SR were allocated six Brush 4s (Class 47) to "assist" with time-keeping problems which were the result of the deteriorating condition of the remaining steam fleet. To list all the services they failed to operate would lead to a detailed statistical list of preposterous proportion. An indication of their unreliability occurred on 14 December 1966 when NONE of the six were working. The sudden short notice replacement which frequently occurred must have been the running foreman's nightmare, i.e. providing not only a fit locomotive but two men *vice* one - but to us enthusiasts it was sheer joy. Although it was never proved I am sure that rumours of sabotage involving bags of sugar and loose fuel caps/covers had some foundation! Having by default travelled with all six at one time or another I was very surprised when, on 10 July 1967, the SR management did not send them back to wherever they came from immediately. Perhaps the most prominent delay was on 3 May 1967 when D1925 failed at Woking whilst working the 05.30 Waterloo to Bournemouth service. Guildford shed eventually sent up Standard 4MT No 76069 which took the Class 1 service forward some two hours late.

Basingstoke – all change

Basingstoke, back then a town of just 30,000 inhabitants, was designated as an "overspill" town for people to move to from London. A futuristic new shopping centre was opened in 1969 and, with a vast increase in commuting to London, is now (2006 census) home to over 80,000. Railway-wise it was an important junction between the LSWR main West of England route and branches in from the Western Region and, of course, to the South Coast. Although by 1966 no passenger services were booked to change traction there, having its own motive power depot with its attendant availability of locomotives and crews made it a natural engine-changing point for trains in trouble - the added advantage of four running lines

was a significant advantage since other services could pass by without the errant train blocking the route completely. The five engine changes I witnessed there (as detailed below) all occurred from December 1966 onwards, thus supporting the theory that the steam fleet, by that date, was in bad shape.

Thursday 5th January: and with D6538 failing on the down through at Winchfield (actual service not noted) Driver King (70A) took 118 minutes to get to Basingstoke on the 17.30 from Waterloo with Standard No 73092 – being passed at Pirbright Junction by the 17.41 ex-Waterloo and at Hook by the 18.00 ex-Waterloo. The Class 5MT was itself a replacement for a failed Brush and although she was blowing off furiously she was changed over for 'West Country' No 34047. No reason was ascertained although it was a known fact that King hated Standards! The train eventually departed 65 minutes late at 19.40.

The second occasion was in the early hours of Thursday 23rd March. The previous afternoon/night I had been chasing MN No. 35012 for the prestige (in the enthusiast's world) of travelling over 1,000 miles with her. I had "negotiated" an early release from my job at Wimbledon and travelled with her on that day's "Royal Wessex" (16 35 ex Waterloo) as far as Dorchester returning, after a local bash in the Poole area, on the Up Mails to Woking, falling asleep en route. Suddenly realising I was at Woking and in a semi-comatose state, I jumped out and dashed over the footbridge, being challenged by BT police as to where I was going at such speed at that time in the morning, and boarded the 02.45 Papers from Waterloo not even knowing what was on the front! At Basingstoke WC No. 34025 *Whimple* was detached and taken on to shed and eventually BoB No. 34052 took over, departing 59 minutes late. Having arrived at Bournemouth at 07.15 breakfast was taken (was it chocolate bars or sandwiches – details not recorded) and I settled down to wait for *United States Lines* which eventually

Stockport's No 70004 'William Shakespeare' waiting departure with the 17 23 'Relief' to Southampton Docks. Having arrived the previous weekend on a rail-tour vice the ailing 'Blue Peter' good use (for the 'puffer nutters' point of view) was made of the loco in a convoluted method to return her home via a northbound banana special from the docks the following day! 16 August 1966.

appeared on a Waterloo service some four hours later – achieving my 1,000 miles with her when passing through Sway.

Four days later, and the fireman on No. 34040, which was working the 10.30 Waterloo to Weymouth, somehow broke/lost his shovel and so an additional stop at Basingstoke was made. Returning to the engine, having successfully obtained a replacement, he noticed a hot box on *Crewkerne's* tender. 25 minutes later and the Class 1 service was taken forward by a hastily prepared No. 75077.

On 22 December '66, whilst I was doing the evening bash to Basingstoke, the "Bournemouth Belle" was noted in the up through platform, full of passengers having their high tea - without an engine! Eventually Standard 5MT No 73018 took the service forward some 60 minutes late.

And finally on 30th May the lightweight 18.38 Salisbury to Waterloo service exchanged a seemingly poor performing Standard No. 75074 for a bigger sister, No. 73043 – with a creditable arrival into Waterloo only 28 minutes late.

Still at Basingstoke but not an engine change: a lifetime ambition was achieved when I (together with several others) genuinely pulled the communication cord because the driver on *Axminster* working the 17.23 Waterloo to Southampton Docks failed to remember that on this night (14 June 1967) the service was advertised as a relief to the 17.30. He was accelerating through the station having been checked outside, but managed to stop with the rear two vehicles still on the platform - continuing after a slight delay with all the butterflies having been reset. Other problems that night for the operating authorities to deal with were twofold. Firstly the Crompton on the 17.09 from Waterloo failed at Woking with a 'burst' fuel tank and soon after a ballast train ripped up the track between Farnborough and Sturt Lane Junction, causing all up stopping services from Farnborough to reverse on to the through line to enable them to continue their eastbound journeys.

Another occasion I was to catch the 17.23 service to Basingstoke was on Tuesday 16th August 1966. Again, the service was intended to act as a relief to the 17.30 Weymouth – on this occasion it was for the benefit of us enthusiasts! After working a railtour through to Waterloo the previous Sunday as a replacement for an ailing *Blue Peter*, 'Britannia' No. 70004 *William Shakespeare* was diagrammed to work the 17.23 Waterloo to Southampton Docks as a somewhat surreptitious method of returning her to the LMR on a banana special the following day. There was a considerable number of enthusiasts working at the Divisional Manager's Office at Worple Road, Wimbledon and it was no surprise when the special traffic notice was issued to see that "Good heavens" the 17.23 that night was to run as a relief to the 17.30 – i.e. call at Basingstoke and Winchester! What the boat passengers thought of the mass invasion by 'anoraks' doesn't bear thinking about. Whilst on the subject of 'Britannias', rumourtrol went into overdrive during late '65 – the 'Britannias' are coming to replace OUR 'Merchant Navies' by June '66. They never arrived.

The oddities

Looking back through my tattered notebooks whilst researching for this article, every now and then I came across an item, noted at the time of being a bit different, that brought all the wonderful memories flooding back. Just about every evening during that last year I, together with many others, travelled from Waterloo on services we knew one day would finish. We were recording history – so every little 'happening' was worth noting. Why – and what - to do with the information was a question that was too far away. Perhaps one day we might document it so that people who had never experienced a steam-operated rush hour could read about. So this paragraph is a reflection of those times and contains individual instances

Deputising for a Brush failure No 34037 'Clovelly' looking resplendent in the afternoon sun was the motive power for the 15 30 to Weymouth on 20th March 1967 - the 15 35 semi to Bournemouth (platform 9) having already succumbed to the replacement TC's.

which made travelling behind steam during that period so memorable. Here goes then. The 17.30 from Waterloo was an express departure at the height of the rush hour – surely such a service would be exempt from delays. It was dieselised in the October of '66 but due to the high failure rate, sometimes causing delayed starts whilst suitable replacement power was found, was returned to steam five weeks later – only to be re-dieselised five weeks later again before eventually being turned over to the inevitable REP & TCs in the March of '67. Twice when I was aboard the train was stopped additionally at Woking, which, from a selfish point of view, was beneficial in allowing me to alight and pursue further 'catches' that night. Severe icing to the third rail one January night decimated the EMU service and the 17.30 was used as a suburban relief service – the other occasion was when the signalman stopped it there because the locomotive's electric headlights were not working. A seven minute station stop was made whilst oil replacements were located. A different delaying reason at Waterloo one August evening amounted to 54 seconds when Driver Hadley jumped off the footplate to rescue his cap from the platform end of No 11!

Back at Woking and *Okehampton*, when working the 17.09, had to set back twice before obtaining clean rail (see photo) resulting in 11 minutes delay. On the 23 November 1966, Woking was the scene of much complaining from bowler hated gentlemen when 76064 worked the 11 coach 18.09 service – Nine Elms having received her the previous day off the 12.59 semi from Bournemouth. Having taken nearly 47 minutes to arrive there with a maximum of 50mph through Surbiton she sat awaiting the requisite boiler pressure, finally departing 22 minutes late. Away from the rush hour but involving sister No. 76058 was an eventful journey on the Down Mails (22.35 ex Waterloo) in the April of '67. Having struggled with

the ten-vehicle train, Driver Sloper stopped at Surbiton for ten minutes, once again, to regain boiler pressure. Eventually reaching Woking in 54 minutes, with a maximum of 48mph en route, a replacement locomotive, in the form of No. 73018, took the Mails away, running 70 minutes late. Woking again: and, having heard through the grapevine (pre-mobile days can you believe!) that *Winston Churchill* was working an Up Semi three days after her funeral exploits I negotiated a long lunch time and travelled down for her. I had several copies of my photograph printed for sale to NON-enthusiasts – she had been on TV after all!

Engineering notices were studied carefully during this period and steam diversions over unusual routes were homed in on. In November '65, No. 35026 took me via the Byfleet/Addlestone curve and Twickenham. A double helping of diversions on one day in June 1966, comprised firstly *Yeovil* on the 03.15 Papers via the Guilford New Line and Pompey Direct (with me being the only passenger on the three coach and two van train) and secondly by doubling back to Woking for *Whimple*, alas with 'Warship' assistance, 'over the Alps' – No.77014 had been used on other occasions!

Unmodified sisters *Bude* and *Exmouth* both suffered from reversing-lever trouble with the said equipment being held in place when at speed – indeed it was very noticeable in the leading coach with what can only be described as "severe judders" often being felt.

That the timings allowed for services in the run up to electrification were slack was proved one Sunday morning when the 11.30 from Waterloo not only stopped at Roundwood signal box to offload coal before reversing at Micheldever over to the up line (SLW in operation) and STILL managed to arrive into Bournemouth 11 minutes early.

Now to the 15.50 from Weymouth – a somewhat slow

'semi' which if one had been bashing all day in Hampshire was prone to being slept on throughout on my journey back to the smoke. An excessively slow 76 minutes between Basingstoke and Woking (23 miles) was awarded me behind *Salisbury* one August evening – the cause being a complete failure of the pneumatic signalling system. *Sir Eustace* (sometimes misheard as useless!) *Missenden* arrived at Basingstoke 40 minutes late on one occasion then stood a further 40 minutes in the platform. The delay was attributable to defective brakes and we eventually departed with 16½ inches of vacuum. This didn't hinder the driver who then obtained a maximum of 79mph through Esher – would the train have been allowed to proceed in today's PC world? The Banbury-allocated Black 5 which laid over at Bournemouth in between Saturday and Monday whilst working the York service was often used by the foreman on London services. Being a Tuesday (21 June1966) it was most surprising to see No. 45349 on the 15.50 service - whilst "new" for a number of my colleagues I had already travelled with the Tyseley-allocated locomotive over ex-GC metals and was not as happy as them!

Finally to the 17.30 from Weymouth which was booked non-stop from Southampton to Waterloo and allocated to Nine Elms crews. It was the depots fastest scheduled service and many a driver changed turns in order to work the 90 mph plus train. A splendid run with Driver Sloper (21 January 1967) was terminated at Walton-on-Thames when *Templecombe* suffered a hot box on her tender. *Aberdeen Commonwealth* was hammered into her grave (06 July 1967) when, having topped Roundwood at 71mph and passed Fleet at 98mph, she was all set the magic ton when apparently a valve cover blew off causing severe internal damage – the crew had to coax her over the remaining 30 miles to Waterloo

Final summary

My travels as documented are obviously from the public side of the railways. The enjoyment achieved was in a relatively clean and comfortable environment. For the train crews it was a different matter. The irregular and unsocial hours worked by train crews amid filthy conditions, both at sheds and on footplates, working with unkempt and unreliable steam locomotives must have been a nightmare. When booking on I have no doubt that the duties/trains they worked sometimes bore little semblance to what their rostered duties should have been. The backbreaking and often monotonous nature of locomotive preparation must have been a major disincentive to many and amid the 60s period of full employment led to obvious staff shortages – in turn causing extra tasks for top link drivers who had expected their steeds to have been fully prepared for them. Was it any wonder that both SR management together with a great many employees looked forward to the cleaner environment that electrification brought them.

However when steam traction ceased, some footplate staff found that the "magic" of the job had disappeared and finding it difficult to adjust left the railway service to pursue a different career – perhaps sating their previous desires as volunteers on what is now, but not known in 1967, a burgeoning preserved railway scene.

I hope I have, through this article, attempted to recreate the atmosphere that I witnessed and enjoyed during those final halcyon days of SR steam and bought back some memories for those readers who were there at the time.

'Etarre' waiting the road for Nine Elms on 16th February 1965. 'Those flats' are in the background.

Shed Visits

Shed	Date	In steam	Dead/Stored	Diesels
70B Feltham	13/08/65 1000	30838/9 75077	30833/7 34012/100 76011/30 80011/9/33/4/89 80140/1	D3273 D6536/56
70E Salisbury	04/04/66 1500	31411/639 33006 34006/26/56/100/8 73065/169 76007/8/12/8/59/67 80152	34076 75066	D807 D1922 D2179 D6505/24/33 15230/1
70F Bmouth	10/12/66 1400	34098/104 35023 41224/30/95/320 73155 76005/11 80032	34024/40 76026 80011/146	Not noted
70F Bmouth	14/01/67 1445	34001/19/44/108 41224/312 76053/66 80011	34024 41230/95/320 76011/26 80032/134	Not noted

Steam Departures from Waterloo - personal

Total	WC/BoB	MN	73xxx	75xxx	76xxx	Others*
358	221 (61%)	96 (26%)	29 (8%)	5	3	5

Steam Arrivals into Waterloo - personal

Total	WC/BoB	MN	73xxx	75xxx	76xxx	Others*
364	209 (57%)	115 (31%	30 (8%)	3	2	5

Steam Locomotive Mileages

Over 1,000	34013/21/36/52/102/8 35003/8/12/3/4/28/30
Over 2,000	35007/23

TOP THREE SERVICES DEPARTED ON

17 09 SX to Basingstoke	102 occasions
17 30 EWD to Weymouth	47 occasions
17 41 SX to Salisbury	26 occasions

TOP THREE SERVICES ARRIVED ON

18 38 EWD from Salisbury (due 20 36)	109
15 50 EWD from Weymouth (due 20 25)	64
17 30 EWD from Weymouth (due 20 51)	43

NAMED SERVICES USED

BOURNEMOUTH BELLE
| 12 30 Waterloo to Bournemouth Central | 8 |
| 16 37 Bournemouth Central to Waterloo | 2 |

Royal Wessex
| 16 35 EWD Waterloo to Weymouth | 8 |

* - others include 31411/639, 33006, 45349, 60024, 60532 & 70004

SX STEAM LOCOMOTIVE DIAGRAMS (Passenger extracts only)   FROM 02/01/67

70A – 105 – LMS 2MT

16 36 MTX Kensington – Clapham Jn
17 06 SX Kensington – Clapham Jn
1736 MTO Kensington – Clapham Jn

70A – 106 Standard 4MT

08 16 SX Clapham Jn – Kensington
08 33 SX Kensington – Clapham Jn
08 46 SX Clapham Jn – Kensington

70A – 113 – Standard 5MT

01 50 Eastleigh - Salisbury
04 40 MSX Waterloo - Salisbury
18 38 SX Salisbury – Waterloo

70A – 134 – WC

17 23 FO Waterloo to Bournemouth Ctl

70A – 135 – WC

08 10 SX Waterloo to Weymouth Q
16 15 SX Weymouth Q – Waterloo

70A – 136 - WC

08 35 SX Waterloo - Weymouth
15 50 SX Weymouth – Waterloo

70A – 137 – WC

10 30 SX Waterloo – Weymouth
17 30 SX Weymouth – Waterloo

70A – 143 – WC

02 30 SX Waterloo – Portsmouth
18 54 SX Waterloo – Basingstoke

70G– 430 – 8P

11 07 SX Bournemouth Ctl - Waterloo
18 30 SX Waterloo – Weymouth

70E – 464 – WC
06 22 SX Bournemouth Ctl – Waterloo
17 09 SX Waterloo – Basingstoke
19 11 SX Basingstoke - Salisbury

CONFESSIONS OF A STEAM AGE SEASON TICKET HOLDER

SX STEAM LOCOMOTIVE DIAGRAMS (Passenger extracts only)   **FROM 27/03/67**

70A – 105 – LMS 2MT
16 36 MTX Kensington – Clapham Jn
17 06 SX Kensington – Clapham Jn
17 36 MTO Kensington – Clapham Jn

70A – 134 – WC
17 23 FO Waterloo to Bournemouth Ctl

70A - 149 – 8P
17 30 SX Weymouth – Waterloo

70A – 106 Standard 4MT
08 16 SX Clapham Jn – Kensington
08 33 SX Kensington – Clapham Jn
08 46 SX Clapham Jn – Kensington

70A – 135 – WC
08 10 SX Waterloo to Weymouth Q
16 15 SX Weymouth Q – Waterloo

70E – 461 - WC
06 49 SX Salisbury - Waterloo
17 09 SX Waterloo o - Basingstoke

70A – 113 – Standard 5MT
01 50 Eastleigh - Salisbury
04 40 MSX Waterloo - Salisbury
18 38 SX Salisbury – Waterloo

70A – 147 – 8P
12 35 SX Bournemouth Ctl - Waterloo
18 54 SX Waterloo – Basingstoke

SX DIESEL LOCOMOTIVE DIAGRAMS (Passenger extracts only)   **FROM 27/03/67**

D90 – Brush 4
On Poole – Reading services

D93 – Brush 4
05 30 SX Waterloo – Bournemouth Ctl
11 07 SX Bournemouth Ctl – Waterloo
15 30 SX Waterloo - Weymouth

D91 – Brush 4
06 22 SX Bournemouth Ctl – Waterloo
12 30 SX Waterloo – Bournemouth Ctl
16 37 SX Bournemouth Ctl – Waterloo
22 35 SX Waterloo – Eastleigh

D92 – Brush 4
06 29 SX Basingstoke - Waterloo
08 30 SX Waterloo – Bournemouth Ctl
12 59 SX Bournemouth Ctl - Waterloo
18 30 SX Waterloo – Bournemouth Ctl
23 37 SX Bournemouth Ctl – Waterloo

Merchant Navy mileages					
No	Name	Runs	Miles	Wdn	Remarks
35003	Royal Mail	17	1,123	07/67	
35005	Canadian Pacific	1	9	10/65	On Mid Hants
35007	Aberdeen Common-wealth	30	2,003	07/67	
35008	Orient Line	21	1,450	07/67	
35010	Blue Star	5	157	09/66	
35011	General Steam Navigation	3	131	02/66	
35012	United States Lines	19	1,332	04/67	
35013	Blue Funnel	21	1,749	07/67	480miles in 3 days – 03/67
35014	Nederland Line	17	1,294	03/67	
35016	Elders Fyffes	1	79	08/65	
35017	Belgian Marine	2	127	07/66	
35019	French Line CGT	1	12	09/65	
35022	Holland America Line	2	31	05/66	
35023	Holland Africa Line	36	2,578	07/67	
35026	Lamport & Holt Line	14	849	03/67	
35027	Port Line	7	358	09/66	5 miles on Blue-bell
35028	Clan Line	22	1,806	07/67	79 on Surrey Hills tour
35029	Ellerman Lines	5	200	09/66	
35030	Elder Dempster Lines	21	1,406	07/67	
Total	**19**	**245**	**16,694**		
Individual year mileages: - 1964=189, 1965=642, 1966=6,783, 1967=6,983, 1994=14, 1997=79					

Loco	Driver	Date	Train	Load	Speed	Location
			Runs at 90 mph and above			
34001	Porter/70A	04/07/67	0245 Wloo/Bomo	3c3v	92	MP31-Hook
				3c2v	98	Wchester Jn
34009	Cummings/70A	16/06/66	1838 Salis/Wloo	4c5v	93	Fleet
34013	De'Ath/Basing	26/09/66	1838Salis/Wloo	5c2v	94	Grateley/Red Post
					90	Oakley/Overton
34015	Gray/70A	15/03/67	1838 Salis/Wloo	5c2v	90	Bwood/Woking
34021	Porter/70A	05/02/67	1803 Bomo/Wloo	10c	90	Fleet/Fboro
34036	Porter/70A	1901/67	1730 Wemo/Wloo	9c2v	90	Winchfield/Fleet
					90	Fleet/Fboro
34037	Davies/70A	05/05/67	1838 Salis/Wloo	5c2v	97	Winchfield/Fleet
34047	Sloper/70A	27/12/66	2230 Wloo/Bomo	7c	90	Wooton/Wallers Ash
34095	Porter/70A	08/07/67	0245 Wloo/Bomo	3c5v	90	Fleet/Winchfield
				3c4v	94	Wooton/Wallers Ash
34098	Porter/70A	17/01/67	1730 Weymo/Wloo	9c2v	95	Woking Jn
					93	Woking
					95	West Byfleet
					90	Weybridge/Hersham
34102	Groome/70A	21/04/67	1838 Salis/Wloo	5c1v	98	Fleet
35003	Enticnap/70A	19/04/67	1838 Salis/Wloo	5c1v	100	Winchfield/Fleet
35003	Groome/70A	20/04/67	1838 Salis/Wloo	6c1v	98	Fleet
					90	Fboro
					93	MP31/Bwood
35003	Hendicott/70A	23/04/67	1130 Wloo/Weymo	6c1v	95	Wallers Ash/Wchester
35003	Chapman/70A	27/04/67	1838 Salis/Wloo	6c1v	101	Winchfield/Fleet
					100	Fleet/Fboro
					100	Bwood
35003	Matthews/70A	04/05/67	1838 Salis/Wloo	8c2v	90	Fleet/Fboro
35003	Burridge/70A	26/06/67	1815 Weymo/Wloo	3c2v	106	Winchfield/Fleet
					101	Fleet/Fboro
35007	Domm/70A	06/07/67	1730 Weymo/Wloo	10c	98	Fleet/Fboro
35012	Parsons/70A	07/04/67	0835 Wloo/Weymo	8c2v	94	Wchester Jn
35013	Porter/70A	18/01/67	1730 Weymo/Wloo	9c2v	93	Winchfield/Fleet
35016		22/05/64	1820 Bomo/Wloo	12c1v	91	Winchfield/Fleet
35023	West/70A	13/09/66	1838 Salis/Wloo	5c5v	90	Fleet
					92	Bwood
35023	Hooker/70A	15/10/66	Rail Tour	8C	101	Hbourne/Andover Jn
35023	Kelly/70A	15/10/66	Rail Tour	8c	90	Grateley/Red Post
					91	Bwood/Woking
35023	Rickman/70A	18/05/67	1838 Salis/Wloo	8c2v	92	Fleet
					94	Bwood/Woking
35028	Porter/70A	16/12/66	1730 Weymo/Wloo	11c1v	91	Basing/Hook
					94	Winchfield/Fleet
35028	Dent/70A	19/06/67	1730 Weymo/Wloo	10c1v	90	Winchfield/Fleet
					91	Fleet/Fboro
35028	West/70A	25/04/67	0835 Wloo/Weymo	8c1v	94	Wallers Ash/Wchester Jn
35030	Sloper/70A	04/02/67	1730 Weymo/Wloo	9c2v	97	Winchfield/Fleet

STRANGERS VISITING NINE ELMS FROM JAN 66 TO THE END (ie **NOT** WC/BoB/MN/41xxx/73xxx/75xxx/76xxx/80xxx/82xxx)

Dates shown indicate entries in running foreman's logbook. This could be individual day visits or staying over a lengthy period. All entries subject to deciphering errors!

Date	Loco		Date	Loco
23/01/66	31639		11&21/06/66	44829
09/02/66	31791		19/06/66	44942
11/03/66	31405		23,24&26/06/66	45349
20/03/66	31639		21/07/66	44710
26&27/03/66	60024		25/07/66	45089
02,04&06/04/66	77014		11&16/08/66	70004
03/04/66	31639		14/08/66	60532
16/04/66	31411 31639		17/09/66	4472
22&24/04/66	31791		19,22&24/09/66	45222
30/04/66	31639 31791		08,10&11/10/66	77014
03/05/66	77014		22/11/66	77014
12&19/05/66	70002		23/12/66	45222
15&22/05/66	45493		05/02/67	77014
			03&04/06/67	4498

TRACTION CHANGES – 01/07/66 TO THE END

I did attempt, having acquired the final Nine Elms running foreman's log book to list all the locomotives working out of Waterloo during the final year. The book, for whatever reasons, did not provide a comprehensive document and even when filling in the gaps, after asking several friends/colleagues for their notations, there were many gaps.

Date	1709 SX Basing	1723 FO Bomo	1730 SX Weym	1741 SX Salis	1800 SX Salis	1809 SX Basing	1822 FO Bomo	1830 SX Weym	1854 SX Salis	1900 SX Exeter
01/07/66	70D WC	70D WC	7OG MN	70E WC	70E WC	70C S5	70D WC	70G MN	70E WC	*Class 42*
05/09/66	70A S5		70F MN							
03/10/66	70G MN	70A S5	*Class 47*		*33& TC*	70A WC			*33 TC*	
14/11/66			70F WC							
28/11/66				*Class 42 a*						70E WC *b*
05/12/66					*33 & TC*				70A WC	
12/12/66			*Class 47*							
02/01/67	70E WC	70A WC		*EMU c*						*Class 42*
06/03/67									70G MN	
27/03/67			*Rep & TC*							
03/04/67								*Class 47*		
01/05/67									70A WC	
08/05/67								*Rep & TC*		
12/06/67	*Class 33*					70A WC				

a - worked 19 00 Waterloo / Exeter forward from Salisbury
b - worked to Salisbury only
c – terminated at Basingstoke

WC - West Country (inc BoB)
MN – Merchant Navy
S5 – Standard 5MT

33 – Crompton (D65xx)   42 – Warship (D8xx)   47 – Brush 4 (D15xx)

~ SOUTHERN MEN ~

It was the staff themselves who really made the railway what is was, as important as - many would say, more so than, the railway machines and infrastructure, although to be fair of course, both were an essential component. But apart from those right at the top of the tree, the individuals below that level are often forgotten, save perhaps by a family whose records consist of a few fading snapshots in an album. A plea then some time ago has resulted in several records passed to us, that on this page with thanks to Robert Latham, reference his Grand-father.

Cecil Joseph Collins Latham was born on 6th August 1882 and entered the service of the South Eastern & Chatham Railway as a Junior Clerk in 1896. As was common for the time he had to proposed for the role, his proposer being Lt. Col. J S Wilson and seconded by Mr F S Bridge.

Some time after this he left these shores and in 1904 was reported as holding the position of Assistant Accountant to the Canadian Northern Railway, aged just 22.

In the same year, 1904, he returned to the South Eastern in the role of Staff Clerk to the Superintendent of the Line at London Bridge. From this time on it was a steady progression, Chief Clerk to the London District Superintendent in 1911, Assistant Superintendent, (Northern District) at Chatham in 1915, Acting District Superintendent, Chatham between 1917 and 1919, and at some stage also, military service: there is a reference to him having been demobbed in 1919. Next came the post of Assistant to the London District Traffic Superintendent and then in 1920, District Superintendent Ashford. He remained in this position until the time of the grouping.

Post grouping, his experience was broadened with the post of Divisional Operating Superintendent at Brighton in 1924 and finally District Traffic Superintendent London Bridge, in 1931, responsible for the Central Division.* He retired from 1st November 1945.

Shortly after his retirement, the *SOUTHERN RAILWAY MAGAZINE* reported a farewell party held at Salisbury on 16th January 1946 at which he was presented with an electric alarm clock and silver condiment set. In retirement, he lived for a time in Cheam before moving to East Stour, where Chinese geese were kept and a large garden cultivated. Family members would travel by means of the 'ACE' west to Salisbury and sometimes change there for Gillingham: being collected by car from one or either station. A final move, to a property with a smaller garden, was to Redlynch.

Left - *Photograph taken during the Brighton & District Ex-Service Railwaymen's Sixth Annual Dinner, held at the Old Ship Hotel, Brighton on 20th November 1930 with Mr Latham in the chair. Others present of note, were S W Smart and J P Maitland. Renowned for his capacity as a speaker, Mr Latham regaled his audience with the story of an Irish stationmaster of verbose inclinations, who having been urged by his Superintendent to be more brief in his communications, reported a derailment thus, " Off again, on again, away again - Flanigan".*

* According to the *SOUTHERN RAILWAY MAGAZINE* for March 1930, Mr Latham was to be appointed one of the five Divisional Superintendents and was based at London Bridge overseeing the Central Division. (London Bridge was also the base for the East Division, whilst others in the same role had their own offices at Waterloo, Southampton West and Exeter. These changes to take place from 31st March 1930.

~CANON STREET 1910~

A Stirling 'F' class 4-4-0 awaiting departure from Cannon Street c1910.
G H Read from the V B Orchard collection

Left - *A1 class 0-6-0T No. 643 'Gypsy Hill' (originally No. 43) on the Bognor Regis branch c1911. Built at Brighton in 1877, it survived until 1925 having during that time run in excess of 1.1 million miles.*

Bottom - *Named after a director of the LBSCR, 'Gladstone' 0-4-2 No. 187 'Philip Rose' waits at Clapham Junction c1910. Built in 1889 it survived into SR days and was withdrawn as No. 2187 in 1930.*

Right - The same train as lower left, seen leaving Clapham Junction.

Bottom - Up passenger train at Surbiton, in charge of 'M7' No. 44, c1910.

From the collection of V B Orchard taken by his Grandfather, G H Read.

*Southern Railway west-country scenes. **Left** - Launceston, 1944. **Bottom** - near Slade reservoir, Ilfracombe.*

THE RAILWAY MEMORIES OF
ARTHUR WESTLAKE

- as first appeared in the Dartmoor Society Magazine and 'The Dartmoor Pony'

Arthur Westlake worked for the Southern Railway, British Railways and British Rail from 1934 to 1983, a period of enormous change on the railways which, among other developments, saw steam locomotives replaced by diesel traction in the South-West by the end of 1965. He began his duties as an engine cleaner at Yeovil Town locomotive shed and, on his retirement, was an Assistant Area Manager based at Okehampton.

Like many other railwaymen, Arthur comes from a railway family; he was born at Halwill Junction, Devon, and of his brothers, Reg was a signalman at Yeovil Junction, Cyril was a shunter at Halwill Junction, Gerald was a driver at Guildford [Surrey] and Holland was a guard, based at Bristol. Arthur's sister Agnes was a signalwoman at Venndown Gates and Meldon Junction. His father was a ganger at Halwill Junction and, even further back, his grandfather had worked at Okehampton Station when the line from Exeter was opened by the London & South Western Railway in 1871.

So it was that the 16-year old Arthur, his railway pedigree already well established, applied to join the Southern Railway He was keen to work on the footplate, but of course had much to learn before this aim could be realised. As was the normal course, this began as a cleaner being the nearest such vacancy at Yeovil in Somerset. Even before this came a check by the SR's Dr George at Salisbury, where one of the most important tests was to state the colour of different flowers to ensure colour blindness would not prevent him distinguishing a night-time signal at red from one at green.

Having successfully passed the medical, he commenced as a cleaner in 1934. This was for 15 shillings for a 48-hour week spread equally over six days. Lodgings cost 12s 6d after which there were additional deductions for trade union and national insurance, at the end of which he was left with just 1/- per week spending money!

He remained as a cleaner for 5 years, recalling the worst part as cleaning out the ash and clinker from the firebox. The long-handled shovel used for this purpose weighed a considerable number of pounds, added to which weight was sometimes as much as a ton of hot clinker to be removed. It was not until 1945 that the first engines with a drop grate, the 'West Country' class came upon the scene.

Having gained experience as a cleaner and accrued also his first firing turns, he was posted as Fireman to Launceston in December 1940. A year later he moved to the Okehampton locomotive shed as a fireman. During this time the men could gain an extra shilling wages by volunteering to cover any type of firing work, as such he worked on troop and munitions workings, such as the once-monthly howitzer trains, on which a howitzer mounted on a rail truck would be hauled to the North Tawton and Sampford Courtenay area. From there, artillery troops would practice by firing at targets set up on Dartmoor a few miles away. On one occasion, Arthur and his driver were on the footplate of a locomotive between Sherborne and Templecombe, when they passed an ammunition train that was being attacked by a German fighter plane. They came through unscathed but, at the next stop found the tender of their locomotive was leaking water through numerous bullet holes. Thankfully, such incidents were rare.

Even though he had not yet become a driver, Arthur was asked to set up improvement classes for the firemen based at Okehampton, Launceston and Bude, the purpose of which was to widen their knowledge of the rules and regulations. The SR had instigated these classes across its whole area, the idea being that there would be a pool of fireman available as drivers for emergency cover. Of the six men in the class, Arthur was the only one to pass – and with a very high mark. Sixty years later he reckoned he could still recite the same rule book.

Promotion to driver came in 1948, still at Okehampton. Arthur was now one of 16 drivers, the depot manpower also consisting of, 16 firemen, two cleaners and two shed staff. Now he would drive passenger and freight trains from his home base to Plymouth, Exeter, Padstow, Bude, Callington and Barnstaple. He was also proud of the fact as a fireman he never once ran short of steam, the clue being, "...to keep the fire hot and not to shovel in too much coal at once."

Although certainly not the largest in size, his favourite was the 'N' class. He recalls an incident where one of these locomotives performed especially well in difficult circumstances. Driving the 1.15pm passenger train from Plymouth, Arthur and his fireman Gerald Smallacombe, stopped at Bere Alston, where there were four parcel vans containing thousands of Mother's Day flowers destined for London. The worried station master approached them, saying that the next available train was not due until 7pm which would mean the flowers missing the service from Okehampton to London and so arriving too late. Arthur and Gerald agreed to hitch the additional four parcel vans on to their train, which already comprised 14 passenger coaches. They realised though they could only achieve this by cutting out unnecessary stops. Thus the stationmaster was asked to phone ahead to each station to ask the staff there to display a green flag if there were no passengers waiting for Arthur's train. At the same time, Arthur and Gerald's guard Tommy went through the train to ascertain which stations they would have to stop at. With the number of stops thus reduced to the minimum, they were able to get their train, now consisting of an unprecedented 18 coaches, to Okehampton on time and so save the stationmaster's skin.

On another occasion, when Arthur and Gerald were working a very heavy train of cattle trucks through Halwill Junction, the sparks from the hard-working engine set light to the roof of a bungalow next to the track.

Arthur remained as driver for eight years and was then promoted to Locomotive Foreman at Okehampton in 1956. He was now in charge of Okehampton along with the smaller sheds at Bude, Launceston and Callington, and wore the foreman's badge of authority – a black bowler hat.

One memorable event of that period was the big freeze of 1962/63, when deep snow blanketed much of the country for many weeks from Christmas 1962, fires being lit underneath locomotives not in use to prevent them freezing. Out on the line locomotives became stuck in deep snow and staff were able to earn extra wages digging them out. However, Arthur noticed that this unforeseen extra overtime was becoming too much of a good thing and set out to stop it. He arranged for three Okehampton locomotives to be steamed and coupled together. These were then taken to each stranded locomotive in turn. With permanent way staff and soldiers clearing the line ahead of the wheels, the combined power of the three was enough to pull each clear. The weather conditions at the time recalled as being similar to those experienced years earlier in 1947.

Unfortunately by this time, rail-borne freight was declining dramatically, particularly on the branch lines. Arthur recalled especially that at one time goods were very varied: wagons of fertiliser, animal feeds and farm implements destined for local merchants were received at local stations, whilst wagons of livestock, meat, milk, pit props and Ambrosia rice puddings were dispatched.

For sometime after the closure of the North Cornwall lines in 1966, Okehampton was tasked as the alternative railhead resulting perhaps in 200 wagons of Fison's fertiliser arriving in a single week. Animal feeds, such as sugar beet nuts and pulp from Bury St Edmunds also arrived. Locally wool and coal were the main commodities dealt with at North Tawton, whilst generally petrol and coal also arrived routinely at most local stations. Sadly all of this business had been in decline following the 1955 national rail strike as customers switched their goods to road hauliers and never returned to the railway. In this way haulage companies such as Messrs. Gregory of North Tawton, Thompson of Moretonhampstead and Passmore of Okehampton prospered.

While he was locomotive shed foreman at Okehampton, the management requested suggestions for improvements from staff. Arthur submitted the idea for the car-train service including a plan for the efficient working of the stock involved. This was adopted between Surbiton and Okehampton and ran from 1958 to 1964. Arthur was paid two guineas for his idea.

As more local lines were closed, mainly due to the plans of Dr Beeching, 28 local stationmasters found themselves redundant. The axe also fell on Arthur, partly because of the demise of steam, but also because fewer services required fewer depots and those services that did continue did not require as many of the smaller sheds - Okehampton was thus closed.

He was fortunate though in that he secured a place as Assistant Area Manager, covering the patch between Okehampton and Kings Nympton, in the process competing against many redundant stationmasters.

Further curtailment came in 1968 when the Plymouth route from Okehampton to Bere Alston closed in 1968 - still regarded as the biggest error of the 'Beeching' closures in the South West. With Okehampton now but a shadow of itself so as the services it once handled, it was to be expected that it too was on borrowed time and indeed passenger workings ceased 1972. Freight though survived, although this was also at one time perceived to be threatened by allowing the projected Okehampton bypass to be built along the favourable alignment of the railway. However, this idea was quietly dropped when it was realised that this would make some 200 workers at Meldon Quarry redundant and would also cut off rail access to a valuable source of railway ballast.

Even at this late stage there were still some dedicated railwaymen, Arthur arranging for large blow lamps to be used to dry a 12-ton consignment of animal feed which had became wet when the bags were left outside in an open wagon. Arthur and his men opened the bags and so dried the feed before rebagging it. Scams over false claims for lost or damaged bags of animal feed were at the time also unfortunately commonplace.

Another scam was also common. It was not unknown for a farmer to put the body of a dead sheep on to the railway and then claim it had been run over by a train. On one such instance, Arthur, knowing that certain stretches of railway fence in the vicinity had been recently renewed, pointed out to the farmer the great athletic capabilities of his sheep in being able to jump over a new railway fence – the claim was quickly dropped!

Scams could also involve passengers, such as when one day 850 troops bound for Okehampton Camp alighted at the station, but with no tickets. Upon investigation it was found that only around half were covered by paid-up travel warrants, the CO at Okehampton Camp made responsible for ensuring the outstanding sum was paid. (Where and how they had borded, likewise how they had managed to avoid ticket checks en-route, were not reported.)

Another claim, soon abandoned, was for a cast iron stove allegedly damaged in transit to Okehampton Station. Unfortunately for the claimant, Arthur himself had been walking along an Okehampton street and witnessed the stove - , delivered and collected from the station in one piece, dropped from

Winter 1962/ 63. No. 31838 is snowed in on Dartmoor but optimistically displaying a Padstow headcode.

the lorry and smashed to pieces on the ground. Such diligence resulted in a commendation from management.

One curious example of freight traffic was the periodic dispatch of 20,000 racing pigeons to Okehampton. These would arrive early on a Sunday morning and the vans would be opened, the birds fed and watered and then released by railway staff. With so many pigeons, the hampers inevitably contained quite a few eggs which were regularly taken away by local people. Arthur made sure the yard gates were locked to keep them out of the way until the birds had been released.

Arthur's quick thinking ultimately helped to preserve Okehampton goods shed. Learning of a plan to demolish it, he promptly arranged for it to be filled with fertiliser bags and set up a 12-month storage rental agreement with the owner. His bosses at Bristol were not best pleased, but the demolition plans were dropped and the shed was saved. It is now used as a Youth Hostel.

Arthur Westlake eventually retired in 1983 but the railway tradition continued with his son Richard, who joined the railway at Okehampton as a cleaner in 1964 and until his own retirement in 2009, was a driver for First Great Western based at Exeter.

This is a slightly abridged version of an article that first appeared in 'The Dartmoor Society' magazine in 2008, compiled by Mike Hedges and Tony Hill from notes during interview / discussion with Arthur Westlake.

It was subsequent reproduced in two parts in 'The Dartmoor Pony' magazine - editor Peter Richie.

Thanks are also due to Russell Burridge - for originally making us aware of the item also to Andre Farmer.

http://dartmoorsociety.com/

http://www.dartmoor-railway.co.uk/

FORD

5 August 1951

Irvine Cresswell

Setting the Scene

Ford station is located on the coastway west line between Brighton and Havant, just west of Arundel Junction and the first station after the convergence of the lines from Arundel, Angmering and Littlehampton. Today the station has two through platforms, with a level crossing at the eastern end of the station with full barriers controlled and supervised by CCTV from Arundel signal box.

In 1951 the station was a typical Southern stopping place with goods yard and sidings, the level crossing having mechanically worked gates from the signal box adjacent to the crossing. In addition to the Down & Up lines there was a Down Loop platform used by trains arriving in the Down direction. Some of these would continue west towards Barnham, although others terminated at Ford and then returned in the Up direction. It was also a busy place, even on a Sunday , no less than 120 workings timetabled of which 42 were Down line stopping services and including four reversals of direction. (The figures for weekdays and Saturdays were even higher at 159 and 171 respectively.)

Train Services

Most trains that stopped at Ford were formed of 4 or 6 coaches electric sets, (combinations of 2BIL and 2NOL units) which would fit in any platform: at the time these were shown as being 474 feet long capable of accommodating a six-car formation..

The Incident

Sunday 5 August was a fine sunny day, remaining as such throughout with good visibility. As was normal for a summer Sunday, some trains were made up to 8 coaches to cope with the expected passenger numbers. The first train involved was the 10.47 am Three Bridges to Bognor Regis via Littlehampton, this was formed of 8 coaches, length 518 ft. and weighing 298 tons. (Both trains were stated to weight the same, the report obviously got one of them wrong!)

It was running two minutes late and in consequence both it and the following Portsmouth train were offered to Signalman R W Arnell at Ford at the same time from Arundel Junction. He accepted the trains in the order they should arrive, viz the Bognor train first. With it (the Bognor train) now stationary in the loop, he then, again quite legitimately, accepted the following Portsmouth train. At this stage the outer home signal, No 47, was at Danger. Signalman Arnell could see this signal from his box and also witnessed the Portsmouth train stop at this point. He had then every reason to believe this train was under full control and consequently cleared the signal to bring the train forward to the inner home signal bracket - also showing danger. He would have realistically expected the train to come to a halt here.

Meanwhile the Bognor train was stationary in the Down Loop platform, any passengers disembarked and loaded as necessary. Unfortunately, due to its length, the rear of the train was foul of the level crossing and also occupied track circuit 'H' that locked the facing points leading from the Down line into the Down Loop. Here at Ford there was an established method of dealing with this situation which would then allow a following Down train to pass on the Down line. This method was both simple and legal and involved reversing the Down Siding trap points, No 18, to allow the associated shunt signal, No 22, to be cleared to authorise the driver to pull forward clear of the level crossing and the associated track circuit. We may assume this was quickly done by Signalman Arnell: the interlocking such that he was unable to clear No 22 until the Inner Home Signal, No 46, was restored to 'On'.

Now though there was some confusions between Porter Harrigan and Guard Eames on the platform, who were in dispute as to who should give authority for the driver to pull forward. There was also some delay attempting to find the owner of a scarf left in one of the carriages. Signalman Arnell reported requesting the Guard to 'hurry up' but clearly to no avail. Bearing in mind this disagreement (- perhaps disagreement may be slightly too strong a word), it is surprising that this issue is not mentioned again in the Inspecting officer's report. Nothing had started to take place before the subsequent accident.

The following train was the 11.17 am Brighton to Portsmouth. This was formed of 6 coaches, 388 ft in length, weighing 298 tons and due to stop in the Down platform. At 11.58 am this train ran by the protecting Inner Home Signal, No 44, at danger and collided with the rear of the stationary Bognor train. As the Bognor train had not yet drawn forward and was thus still standing on track circuit 'H', this meant the crossover No 32 was still set for the movement into the loop.

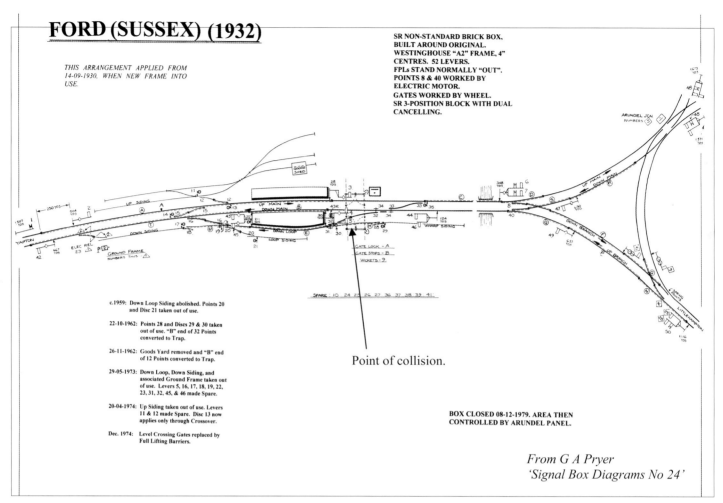

FORD (SUSSEX) (1932)

THIS ARRANGEMENT APPLIED FROM
14-09-1930, WHEN NEW FRAME INTO
USE.

SR NON-STANDARD BRICK BOX,
BUILT AROUND ORIGINAL.
WESTINGHOUSE "A2" FRAME, 4"
CENTRES. 52 LEVERS.
FPLs STAND NORMALLY "OUT".
POINTS 8 & 40 WORKED BY
ELECTRIC MOTOR.
GATES WORKED BY WHEEL.
SR 3-POSITION BLOCK WITH DUAL
CANCELLING.

GATE LOCK - A
GATE STOPS - B
WICKETS - 9

c.1959: Down Loop Siding abolished. Points 20 and Disc 21 taken out of use.

22-10-1962: Points 28 and Discs 29 & 30 taken out of use. "B" end of 32 Points converted to Trap.

26-11-1962: Goods Yard removed and "B" end of 12 Points converted to Trap.

29-05-1973: Down Loop, Down Siding, and associated Ground Frame taken out of use. Levers 5, 16, 17, 18, 19, 22, 23, 31, 32, 45, & 46 made Spare.

20-04-1974: Up Siding taken out of use. Levers 11 & 12 made Spare. Disc 13 now applies only through Crossover.

Dec. 1974: Level Crossing Gates replaced by Full Lifting Barriers.

SPARE: 10 24 25 26 27 36 37 38 39 41.

Point of collision.

BOX CLOSED 08-12-1979. AREA THEN
CONTROLLED BY ARUNDEL PANEL.

From G A Pryer
'Signal Box Diagrams No 24'

Had the draw forward move been made, this would have cleared, the track circuit instead locking the points in that position.

It was considered in the Accident Report that the driver of the approaching Portsmouth train only realised his error at the very last moment, but that he just had time to instinctively put the controller in the reverse position. The collision speed was estimated to be 18mph; unfortunately this could not be confirmed with the driver of the Portsmouth train as he lost his life in the collision. In addition, eight passengers lost their lives, including a mother and her two daughters.

As can be gleaned from the photographs, there was considerable damage to both the rear coach of the Bognor train and the also the leading coach of the Portsmouth working. Both of these consisting of a wooden framed body having steel body panels on steel underframes with standard 3-link couplings. The pictures show the damage to the coaches even with a comparatively slow collision.

The Signalling

The signals and points were controlled from the signal box adjacent to the level crossing; the interlocking of the equipment was achieved with a combination of electric and mechanical means that would protect trains and road users from a dangerous situation.

The 10.47 am Three Bridges to Bognor train had been signalled into the Down Loop, which required 32 points reversed and also locked by Facing Point Lock 34. This then allowed No 46 (Down Loop Home) signal to be cleared. At the west end of the platform, No 22 (Shunt to the Down Siding) signal was locked in the danger position to prevent confusion and stop a train running straight into the siding. The Bognor train thus quite legitimately came to a stand at No 45 (Down Loop Starter) signal, but because of the train length Track Circuit 'H' remained occupied. This in turn prevented 32 points from being moved, the signalman had though returned 46 signal to danger.

The following 11.17 am Brighton to Portsmouth train could be safely signalled as far as 44/46 signal, the driver would have had an earlier warning of this situation as the relevant Distant Signal (No 48) would have been in the 'On' position.

Indeed up to this point Motorman Sherwood had been behaving perfectly normally, evidence of this coming from Guard Knight on the train. He recalled his train being held for 2½ minutes for signals at Arundel Junction and then for a further half minute at the Outer Home Signal, No 47. He observed through his periscope this signal clear but then stated he began recording the delays in his train register and so did not see the position of the inner home signal as they approached Ford. This lack of attention, at what the Inspecting Officer regarded as a crucial point, was criticised in the report.

74

The proximity of the Naval Air Station at Ford: nowadays the site is used as an open prison, market, and industrial estate, may have contributed to the existence of the various arial views.

Interestingly, nowhere in the official report is there reference to the stock involved and instead detail is found in the 'Railway Observer'. According to the 'Railway Observer' both trains comprised 'BIL' units although from the roof ventilator positions one may even have been a 'NOL' unit. The 'R.O' gives the set numbers, respectively from the front as: Bognor working, units 2101, 2150, 2052 and 2069. Portsmouth train, units 2160, 2029 and 2048. Understandable it was sets 2069 and 2160 that took the brunt of the impact, ingress into each having taken place over a distance of some 40 feet, with lesser damage to 2052 and 2029. The signal post at the Brighton end of the Down platform was also twisted and quickly replaced.

The Aftermath

In addition to the 9 people that lost their lives, 47 were injured. The traction supply to the down line immediately isolated as the result of the short circuit caused by the incident. Help was quickly on the scene. Within 10 minutes Police, Fire-Brigade and Medical Staff began to arrive and a casualty station and lost property office was set up at the nearby Royal Naval Air Station. It was from here that the more seriously injured were ferried to hospital.

Locally, train services were terminated at Littlehampton and Barnham, a fleet of double-deck buses used between the two stations. As this was peak holiday time, it was reported that large queues formed very quickly, but that the buses dealt with the people expediously.

With current to the third rail on the down side cut-off, that appertaining to the up side was isolated from the Havant control room within two minutes, at the request of the signalman.

The Brighton and Fratton breakdown cranes attended the incident and were on site by early afternoon. Fortunately there was little or no track damage and the debris was cleared for normal services to be resumed on the up line at 5.45 pm and fully by 8 o'clock the same day.

An inquest was opened on the following Wednesday, where Mr Jones of The Railway Executive stated that the railway must accept full legal responsibility for the incident, as it was considered that the driver had run by signals in the 'Danger' position. Clearly this was the only course of action possible by the RE although it was still a little surprising that such an admission was in fact made so quickly. This decision by the Executive was no doubt based upon evidence that subsequent examination and comment revealed the driver of the Portsmouth train to have had no underlying health condition whilst the brakes and signalling were all in order and there were no outside factors involved. It appears that at the very last moment Motorman Sherwood of the Portsmouth train must have realised his error as the control key was found in the reverse position although the brakes had not been applied. This was confirmed by a witness waiting in his car at the crossing, who stated the position of the signals as being at Danger and that there was no sudden rush of air as would have been expected from the brakes; his car was subsequently showered with debris.

The Ministry of Transport report, compiled by Brigadier C A Langley, was published on 25 October 1951. Having assessed the evidence, there was but one conclusion possible: driver error. Perhaps even brought about by Motorman Sherwood seeing the actual platform clear so assuming that the route was properly set. The sighting of the Inner Home Signal was not considered a mitigating factor. (It must be recalled the Bognor train was not actually stood on the main line, but as reported, because of its position, the crossover was still reversed.)

In his recommendations, Brigadier Langley advised lengthening the platform at Ford and commented upon the progress already being made toward the constructions of stronger rolling stock. The last sentence of his report though accepted the enviable, "The coaches of the type involved in this accident have, however, many more years of useful life and premature scrapping cannot be justified".

The misshapen remains of the rear-most driving trailer of the Bognor train: 2069, and the front of the Portsmouth working, 2160. The damaged signal is also clearly visible. Although not mentioned as such, it is very likely the fatalities occurred in these two vehicles.

Above - Quieter times at Ford. Electric No. 20003 on an eastbound goods, 9 July 1955.
Below - between Arundel Junction and Littlehampton Junction, 'Q' class No. 30536 has charge of Mid Sussex line goods working, 8 March 1956.

Both - Ted Gamblin

THE KENT COAST ELECTRIFICATION

PHASE 1

In the first part of the article on Phase 1 of the Kent Coast Electrification (KCE), which appeared in Issue No.5, **Jeffery Grayer** *recalled the variety of new motive power introduced. In this second part the consequent effects on local steam traction and upon coaching stock are examined.*

The year 1958 was to be the last full summer of Kent Coast steam working and a wide variety of steam motive power was in evidence, ranging from 'Merchant Navy' and Bulleid Light Pacifics, 'King Arthurs', 'Schools', Standard Class 4s and 5s, Maunsell moguls and a range of inside-cylinder 4-4-0s supplemented by C class goods and H class tank engines. The South Eastern Division's two 'Britannia' Pacifics, Nos. 70004 and 70014, had returned to the Midland Region in May 1958 leaving the "Golden Arrow" and the heavy boat trains in the hands of Stewarts Lane's trio of 'Merchants', Nos. 35001/15/28. Maunsell 4-4-0s were active on summer Saturday express work right up to the eve of electrification in June 1959 and, in the hands of such masters of their art as 73A driver Sammy Gingell, they continued to put in sterling performances until the very last.

However, passengers were to experience frustrating times in the run up to electrification, with the inevitable delays following from engineering works in connection with the introduction of the new motive power. Schedules were not adjusted to reflect these disruptions and consistency of timekeeping was also adversely affected by the practice of indiscriminately rostering 4-4-0s, 4-6-0s and 4-6-2s to many of the principal trains.

For the record, the last scheduled steam locomotive to work on the Chatham mainline was 'L1' 4-4-0 No. 31753, which brought the 20.52 from Victoria into Dover Marine on Sunday 14th June 1959. The last scheduled steam-hauled Ramsgate-Victoria train left at 20.35 with No. 34001 *Exeter* in charge, both locomotives being decorated with wreaths and accompanied by much whistling upon departure from other locomotives in the vicinity. The "Night Ferry" was the first public passenger service to be worked electrically, one week in advance of the changeover, from 8th. June. By Friday of that week, however, the electric locomotive had been temporarily withdrawn with brake trouble and steam was again in charge. On the morning of 13th June the up train was divided, the sleeping-car portion coming up to town with the usual Bulleid Pacific and 4-4-0 combination, whilst the non-sleeping portion was in the charge of 'D'1 No. 31505. That same evening the down "Night Ferry" was taken by No. 35015 *Rotterdam Lloyd* which also brought in the up train on 14th June, after which electric locomotives resumed this duty. On 24th June the 16.04 from Folkestone (ex-Calais) arrived at Victoria with No. 34087 *145 Squadron* and No. 34017 *Ilfracombe* at the head.

Steam working of any sort ceased almost completely between Gillingham and Margate following electrification, freight being handled by E5000 types and Cromptons with diesel shunters in attendance at Sittingbourne and Faversham, although one steam shunting turn remained initially, at Gillingham. A number of Light Pacifics and 'Schools' hung on at 73A for Continental and summer inter-regional train haulage until June 1961 and the energising of the Tonbridge and Minster lines. As Appendix 1 shows, three sheds lost their steam allocation completely - Gillingham, Faversham and Ramsgate - although derelict 'D' Class No. 31501 remained in use on carriage shed heating duties at Ramsgate shed, the locomotive having been withdrawn in 1953 from Hither Green. Bricklayers Arms shed remained open to cater for its rump of Central Section work with a 17 engine stud until the switch to the summer timetable in 1962 when its residual work was farmed out to 73A, Norwood Junction and Brighton. Stewarts Lane did not close to steam until June 1963.

The winter of 1959 saw a number of difficulties involving points problems, signalling failures and breakdowns of motive power, the new electric locomotives being particularly unreliable, with a substantial number to be seen at Stewarts Lane under repair. The elderly 4-4-0s which the SE Division had been very quick to get rid of, on paper at least, to the Western Section were still active on local trains particularly in the Tonbridge area as late as October. The electric and diesel locomotives did not initially prove to be the success that was hoped and on one day in November no fewer than nine electric locomotives were out of service, steam having to come to the rescue on a number of occasions; for example on 11th November when No. 31856 worked the down coal empties to Snowdown colliery in place of the usual diesel. On 12th November four steam locomotives were observed at Sittingbourne, Nos. 33030 and 31542 on down goods workings, No. 33031 on an up goods and No. 30922 *Marlborough* on an up van train. The following day a 'C' and two 'N' class moguls put in appearances at Sittingbourne. An evening parcels from the North Kent line was worked by No. 34027 *Taw Valley* on 11th December, in place of the usual electric locomotive. D1 No. 31487 worked the end-of-term school train from Cranbrook to Charing Cross on 15th December.

A considerable number of the locomotives displaced by the KCE were, on paper at least, transferred *en masse* to

Opposite page - The new order: as intended. E5000 types on the prestige 'Golden Arrow' were equally at home working freight. However, as recounted in the text, things did not always go as smoothly as intended.

The old order at London Bridge, 12 June 1957. Arriving with the 6.29 am from Ramsgate is No. 34075 '264 Squadron'.

Nine Elms in the summer of 1959. Allowing for a few transfers away, the net increase virtually doubled the previous allocation at 70A. The transfers included the entire complement of 'L1', 'E1' and 'R1' classes, 25 'C' class, 17 'L's, 9 'D1's, 8 'H's, 2 'O'1s, 10 'Schools', 9 'Standard class 5's and 3 'Merchant Navies'. Apart from the latter two classes, which were probably welcomed, it was hard to imagine that gainful employment could be found for the remainder. However, a niche had been found in 1957, following the Hastings Line dieselisation, for some of the 'Schools' class in operating Saturday through trains from Waterloo to Lymington, at least as far as Brockenhurst, as detailed in the article contained in the Preview Issue of *Southern Way*. Full details of the KCE transfers are shown in Appendix 2. Two lines of condemned locomotives witnessed outside Ashford Works early in August contained many which had theoretically been transferred to Nine Elms.

All the South Eastern Division 'King Arthurs' moved to the Western Section, four going to Feltham. Thus Stewarts Lane, which had already been denuded of its 4-6-0s and Heavy Pacifics, was left to cope with peak continental and inter-regional traffic with just Light Pacifics and 'Schools'. However, it was unlikely that all of the transfers actually took place and nothing like the full number of transferees had put in

an appearance at 70A by mid-July, no 'Merchant Navies' and few of the light Pacifics having by that time been transferred. Only four Class 5s were noted, though several 'Schools' and 'Arthurs' had arrived by this date.

The 'L1's arrived at Nine Elms late in June 1959 and Nos.31754/85/86/89 appeared regularly for a fortnight on a Reading van train duty but subsequently were replaced by the more usual moguls. No. 31786 handled the Surbiton - Nine Elms goods for a brief period in the summer and 'D'1 No. 31735 took a turn on the Waterloo – Basingstoke empties. Newly transferred C class No. 31054 had charge of the Nine Elms breakdown train on 11th. September in Wimbledon sidings, whilst new acquisition 'H' class No. 31552 was noted initially on Clapham Junction ecs duties although this Wainwright tank was subsequently put into store. In mid-July the following ex SE Division locomotives were observed at 70A – Nos. 30796, 30909, 30910/11/16/23, 31033, 31505/52, 31753 /4/8/68/70/75/85/86/87/89, 31812, 73041/88/89. Five D1s, Nos. 31246/494/509/545/727, which had been nominally transferred to Nine Elms were in fact to be found in store at Feltham on 5th July, whilst 'E1' No. 31497 was in store at Reading South shed. Dumped at Brighton were 'C' class No. 31242 and 'L1's Nos. 31759 and 31782 together with 'L' Class Nos. 31764, 31765 and 31780. In view of the shortage of space at 75A, they were moved into the disused boiler shop of Brighton Works in July. There they remained until shortly before Christmas 1960 when the 'C' and two of the 'L1's were drawn out of the Works in anticipation of extra holiday parcels traffic. However, in the event they were never used for this purpose and were despatched to Ashford for scrapping a couple of months later. There was a plan apparently to use Fratton depot as a storage facility for redundant 'L1' and 'H' classes but this never came to fruition although a couple of 'L1's did make it there. Following attention to safety valves and tender axleboxes No. 31753 journeyed to Fratton ostensibly for service on the Southampton line. Not much use was made of it and by May 1960 it had returned to the fold at Nine Elms. Another example, No. 31757, did spend some time in Fratton depot roundhouse, in company with No. 30777 *Sir Lamiel*, and, all but forgotten, lingered on to outlive other members of its class by more than a year, not being scrapped at Eastleigh Works until March 1963.

Most of the ex-Kentish locomotives at 70A remained in store for the winter period but a few were utilised. No. 31753, the only active 'L1', and 'C' class Nos. 31271 and 31720 were seen on Sundays with engineers trains at Clapham Junction and No. 31552 was used as shed pilot at 70A. Christmas parcels traffic brought several ex-SECR locomotives out of store such as No. 31545 working a Walton – Nine Elms van train; No. 31509 took the 10.52 Waterloo-Reading parcels; and No. 31768 was on the Waterloo-Richmond via Kingston parcels formed of special Maunsell vehicles. 'H' class No. 31552 was working ecs at Waterloo on 9th. January 1959. In the early part of 1959 steam locomotives continued to put in frequent if not regular appearances on the newly-electrified lines, either as replacements for diesel or electric traction or on extra turns. Goods and parcels traffic on the Sheerness branch remained steam-hauled. Newly repainted 'D1' No. 31489 brought the 11.30 ex- Ramsgate into Charing Cross on February 2nd. It was still possible to experience a non- stop run behind steam on the Tonbridge – Ashford racing section as the 07.24 London Bridge – Ramsgate was worked on 15th. March 1959 by No. 31739 taking just 32.25 minutes for this 26.5 mile section.

In summary the transfer of ex-Kentish steam was something of an embarrassment to receiving sheds, particularly 70A, and little work was found for the majority of locomotives. It can be seen from Appendix 1 that a number of those that were transferred were in fact scrapped in short order and often recipient sheds were quick to pass on some of their surplus motive power as soon as was decently possible, a month or two after receipt. For example, Nine Elms got rid of four 'C' Class, including two which were given a new lease of life by being transferred to Guildford shed and one which broke new ground by being transferred to Feltham in place of withdrawn 700 Class No. 30353. They also rid themselves of two 'Schools', one 'H' tank, one 'D1' to Eastleigh, and all four 'E1's which went as far west as Salisbury to replace 'T9's working on local services to Bournemouth, Eastleigh and Southampton by the end of August. Similarly Brighton divested itself of four of its

H class very quickly, although with the influx of this type all push-pull workings on the Steyning and Cranleigh lines were diagrammed to be worked by them, as Brighton locomotive crews found them easier to handle than the 'M7's used previously.

The transfer of former South Eastern 4-4-0s to Salisbury and Eastleigh was particularly noteworthy to local enthusiasts but not appreciated by men raised on LSWR machines such as Drummond's 'T9's. Their stay at 72B did not last long, for by April 1960 two had been transferred to Stewarts Lane and two to Bricklayer's Arms. Eastleigh's 'D1', No. 31735, was, upon receipt at 71A, immediately placed into store until Christmas when it performed on local parcels workings. Following the festive break it was returned to store until the following Christmas, hardly a high utilisation factor! Over the 1960 Christmas period it was seen on the 10.57 Salisbury-Portsmouth vans working and the 21.48 Fratton-Eastleigh goods whilst early in the New Year it took over 'Q' class goods duties which included shunting Woolston Yard. It was last noted in steam on 30 March 1961 being withdrawn the following month with a very creditable 1.9 million miles under its belt.

What of the steam-hauled coaching stock ? In anticipation of the KCE and the cascading down of vehicles, a general withdrawal order was made in September 1958 covering most stock over 30 years old, thus condemning much of the Maunsell-designed stock that had been the pride of the newly formed SR including the narrow-bodied 'Thanet' and 'Hastings' types as well as the matchboarded 'Continentals' of SECR design and all pre-grouping survivals. The region's 2900 coaches were to be reduced to 1700 by 1962 of which 1300 would be Bulleid or Standard types. By 1962 only some 400 out of 1560 pre-1938 loco-hauled corridor vehicles would remain in service. Amongst coaches broken up at the scrapping facility based at Newhaven in November 1958 were BSKs S4055S and S4056S, CK S5147S from Set 445 built about 1927 and latterly allocated to the S&D line, "Ironclad" BFK S7711S built in 1922 and used for Southampton Boat Train services and SE&CR matchboard-panelled BFK S7753S. These were joined in January 1959 by CK S5522S and S5541S two of the original Kent Coast corridor vehicles built in 1924.

'Thanet' set 424 was condemned at the end of May 1959 and 41 other vehicles of 'Thanet', 'Ironclad' and 'Continental' types from sets 211, 423, 460 had arrived to await condemnation by 16 June at Ardingly, on the branch from Haywards Heath to Horsted Keynes, which had, ironically, previously been used to store the new electric units. (See feature on Ardingly electric stock storage in *SW No. 5* and the comprehensive listing of redundant coaching stock in *SW No. 7*). At the end of July 1959 about 200 coaches were parked on the down line between Horsted Keynes and Ardingly, in Horsted Keynes station itself and beyond. About 30 more coaches were at Gatwick, 20 at Hassocks and several more were to be found at Seaford and at Newhaven. The famous "Margate Miners" train set No 346, always a repository of ancient vehicles and latterly made up of SECR seconds with a

'Continental' brake, was replaced by six second-class vehicles, four "Thanet" coaches, a Maunsell vehicle and an "Ironclad". The KCE scheme was officially quoted as rendering redundant some 400 coaches: however a large number had already been taken out of service in anticipation during the winter of 1958/59. Broadly, the redundant vehicles comprised the remaining 'Ironclads' except for a few still in service on the South Western Division, the remaining 'Continental' matchboarded stock, except for a few retained for boat train services, the 'Thanet' stock, the 'Restriction 1' Boat SO vehicles and about half the "Hastings" stock, most of which had remained in service after dieselisation of the Hastings route. A number of SR standard restriction 4 vehicles of pre-1929 vintage were also withdrawn. About 100 vehicles, many loose SK, SO and FK types, were transferred from the SE to the SW Division and a number of Bulleid and Standard coaches were transferred to the Oxted line. Among SE sets disbanded were the business formations 265/6/7 and 473. The SE coaching allocation subsequently consisted mainly of Bulleid and Standard vehicles, whilst most of the remaining Maunsell stock was concentrated on the SW Division. About 30 corridor vehicles were fitted with dual heating arrangements as electric locomotives could not provide steam-heating for use on SE section boat trains. A considerable proportion of the surplus coaching stock was despatched to Newhaven for breaking-up during the winter of 1958/59. Of the remainder, most were disposed of to Maze Hill, Blackheath and Eardley. Other redundant stock was berthed at Headcorn, Grove Park, Martin Mill and Canterbury with four sets, totalling 41 vehicles, being sent to Horsted Keynes to await onward transfer to Newhaven.

Interestingly, in view of complaints regarding the rough riding of the new electric stock in service, 'Schools' Class No. 30917 operated some special test runs between Hove and New Cross Gate on 9th March 1960 with a 4-BEP buffet car coach S69008 marshalled in a six coach formation of steam stock, the buffet car being specially fitted with vacuum brake pipes for these trips. Whilst the new electric services were certainly faster, the comfort of the old steam-hauled carriage stock could not be equalled even after the fitting of new Commonwealth bogies to the EMUs for Phase II of the KCE. Even then G Freeman Allen considered that "***The riding of all Southern main line EMUs is still half-a-century adrift of the quality found on any main line north of the Thames***" !

In conclusion it can be appreciated that the effects of the KCE on both steam locomotives and coaches was far reaching, being the catalyst for the withdrawal of much vintage coaching stock and shortening the active lives of the more elderly steam types.

The old and the perhaps not quite so new at Orpington. Schools 30900 'Eton', built in 1930, passing a 1925 '3SUB' unit augmented to four cars with the addition of a Bulleid coach. Ironically, it was the newer steam locomotive that was under threat.

Arthur W V Mace: Milepost 92½ / Corbis

Snow Hill (Holborn Viaduct). 'C' class No. 31102 awaiting a signal. This was a Bricklayers Lane locomotive which survived until May 1960.

FAVERSHAM 73E (Became Diesel Locomotive Depot only)			
Class	No	Transferred to	With-drawn
C	31242	70A	9/61
C	31255	73F	9/61
C	31256	73F	7/61
C	31268	70A	4/62
C	31298	70A	11/60
C	31481	70A	11/61
C	31714	73A	7/61
C	31715	73A	11/61
D1	31494	70A	8/60
D1	31505	70A	9/61
D1	31509	70A	5/60
H	31503	70A	8/59
L	31765	73H	2/61
L	31766	73H	2/61
L	31768	73H	12/61
N	31850	72A	1/64
N	31852	72A	9/63
U1	31892	70B	11/62
U1	31893	70B	12/62
U1	31903	73J	12/62
Ivatt	41308	73F	
Ivatt	41309	73F	
Ivatt	41310	73F	
Ivatt	41311	73F	
Ivatt	41312	73F	
Ivatt	41313	73F	
Total 26			

GILLINGHAM 73D - 73J from 6/59 (Became stabling point during summer with 4 x Q1 and 3 x H supplied by Tonbridge			
Class	No	Transferred to	With-drawn
C	31037	70A	2/61
C	31112	70A	4/62
C	31227	70A	10/59
C	31229	70A	10/61
C	31297	70A	9/59
C	31495	70A	3/61
C	31510	70A	6/62
C	31576	70A	11/59
C	31579	70A	10/61
C	31682	70A	10/61
C	31683	70A	6/59
C	31684	70A	10/61
C	31720	70A	10/61
H	31161	75A	11/61
H	31308	75A	12/62
H	31322	75A	4/61
H	31512	75A	6/61
H	31518	75A	1/64
H	31548	75A	8/59
L1	31785	70A	1/60
L1	31786	70A	2/62
L1	31787	70A	1/61
N	31815	73C	5/63
N	31816	73C	1/66
Total 24			

RAMSGATE 73G - 73F (Became stabling point only, the maximum requirement being 6 x WC, 3 x LM Class 4 tank, 3 Standard Class 2 tank, 1 x N. Closed 12/12/1960)			
Class	No	Transferred to	With-drawn
C	31004	70A	11/61
C	31245	70A	8/59
C	31252	70A	7/59
C	31271	70A	7/63
C	31595	70A	7/63
H	31324	70A	7/62
H	31326	70A	10/61
H	31500	70A	6/61
L	31764	73H	2/61
L	31775	73H	8/59
L	31779	73H	7/59
L	31780	73H	7/60
L	31781	73H	6/59
V	30910	70A	11/61
V	30911	70A	12/62
V	30912	70A	11/62
V	30913	70A	1/62
V	30914	75A	7/61
V	30916	70A	12/62
V	30917	70A	11/62
V	30918	70A	10/61
V	30919	70A	2/61
V	30920	73A	11/61
V	30921	73A	12/62
V	30922	73A	11/61
WC	34016	73B	6/64
WC	34017	73B	10/66
WC	34021	73B	7/67
WC	34022	73B	9/66
WC	34025	73B	8/64
WC	34026	73B	7/67
WC	34027	73B	9/64
WC	34037	73B	
WC	34078	73B	
Class 2	84025	73F	
Class 2	84026	73F	
Class 2	84027	73F	
Class 2	84028	73F	
Class 2	84029	73F	
Total 39			

Appendix 1.
Final Steam Allocations, June 1959.

Appendix 2

Class	No	From	To	Withdrawn	Class	No	From	To	Withdrawn
			Steam Locomotive Transfers Resulting From KENT COAST ELECTRIFICATION May / June 1959						
C	31242	73E	70A	9/61	D1	31727	73F	70A to 71B 8/59	3/61
C	31255	73E	73F	9/61	D1	31735	73B	70A	4/61
C	31256	73E	73F	7/61	D1	31743	73A	73B	2/60
C	31268	73E	70A	4/62	D1	31749	73A	73B	11/61
C	31298	73E	70A	11/60	H	31503	73E	70A	8/59
C	31481	73E	70A to 73H 8/59	11/61	H	31161	73D	75A TO 75E 6/59	11/61
C	31714	73E	73A	7/61	H	31308	73D	75A	12/62
C	31715	73E	73A	11/61	H	31322	73D	75A	4/61
C	31037	73D	70A to 70C 7/59	2/61	H	31512	73D	75A TO 73J 6/59	6/61
C	31112	73D	70A to 73H 7-8/59	4/62	H	31518	73D	75A TO 73J 6/59	1/64
C	31227	73D	70A	10/59	H	31548	73D	75A	8/59
C	31229	73D	70A	10/61	H	31324	73G	75A	7/62
C	31297	73D	70A	9/59	H	31326	73G	70A TO 73H 7-8/59	10/61
C	31495	73D	70A	3/61	H	31500	73G	70A	6/61
C	31510	73D	70A	6/62	H	31266	73J	70A	10/60
C	31576	73D	70A	11/59	H	31522	73F	75A TO 75e 6/59	1/63
C	31579	73D	70A	10/61	H	31552	73A	70A	11/61
C	31682	73D	70A	10/61	H	31553	73B	70A	6/61
C	31683	73D	70A	6/59	L	31760	73J	70A	6/61
C	31684	73D	70A	10/61	L	31762	73J	70A	2/60
C	31720	73D	70A	10/61	L	31763	73J	70A	4/60
C	31004	73G	70A	11/61	L	31764	73G	70A	2/61
C	31425	73G	70A	8/59	L	31765	73E	70A	2/61
C	31252	73G	70A	7/59	L	31766	73E	70A	2/61
C	31271	/3G	70A	7/63	L	31768	73E	70A	12/61
C	31592	73G	70A	7/63	L	31770	73J	70A	11/59
C	31033	73C	70A	3/60	L	31771	73J	70A	12/61
C	31054	73C	70A to 70B 7/59	8/60	L	31773	73J	70A	8/59
C	31061	73C	70A to 70C 7/59	7/61	L	31775	73G	70A	8/59
D1	31494	73E	70A	8/60	L	31776	75A	70A	2/61
D1	31505	73E	70A	9/61	L	31777	75A	70A	9/59
D1	31509	73E	70A	5/60	L	31778	75A	70A	8/59
D1	31145	73A	70A	10/61	L	31779	73G	70A	7/59
D1	31246	73F	70A	3/61	L	31780	73G	70A	7/60
D1	31247	73B	70A	7/61	L	31781	73G	70A	6/59
D1	31545	73A	70A	3/61	N	31408	73A	73F	6/66

Another one that made it to Nine Elms - just. 'D1' 31145 poses alongside 'L1' 31756 with another interloper, an 'H' tank on the right.

colspan table									

Steam Locomotive Transfers Resulting From KENT COAST ELECTRIFICATION May / June 1959

Class	No	From	To	Withdrawn	Class	No	From	To	Withdrawn
N	31409	73A	73F	10/62	N	31861	73C	75B	5/63
N	31413	73A	73H	6/64	N	31870	73B	75B	4/64
N	31414	73A	73H	11/62	N	31871	73B	75B	11/63
N	31810	73A	73H	3/64	N	31872	73B	75B	5/63
N	31811	73A	70C	7/65	U1	31890	73B	75A	6/63
N	31812	73A	70C	7/64	U1	31891	73B	75A	3/63
N	31850	73E	72A	1/64	U1	31892	73E	70B	11/62
N	31851	73B	72A	9/63	U1	31893	73E	70B	12/62
N	31852	73E	72A	9/63	U1	31894	73A	70B to 73A 6/59	12/62
N	31853	73B	72A	9/64	U1	31895	73A	70B to 73A 6/59	12/62
N	31815	73D	73C	5/63	U1	31896	73J	73A	12/62
N	31816	73D	73C	1/66	U1	31899	73B	73A	12/62
N	31860	73C	72A	11/63	U1	31900	73B	73A	12/62

Class	No	From	To	Withdrawn	Class	No	From	To	Withdrawn
\multicolumn{10}{c}{**Steam Locomotive Transfers Resulting From KENT COAST ELECTRIFICATION May / June 1959**}

Class	No	From	To	Withdrawn	Class	No	From	To	Withdrawn
U1	31901	73B	73J	6/63	V	30912	73G	70A	12/62
U1	31902	73B	73J	11/62	V	30913	73g	70A	1/62
U1	31903	73E	73J	12/62	V	30914	73G	75A	7/61
U1	31904	73A	73J	11/62	V	30916	73G	70A to 75A 7/59	12/62
U1	31905	73A	73J	12/62	V	30917	73G	70A to 75A 7/59	11/62
U1	31906	73A	73J	12/62	V	30918	73G	70A	10/61
U1	31907	73A	73J	12/62	V	30919	73G	70A	2/61
Ivatt	41308	73E	73F		V	30920	73G	73A	11/61
Ivatt	41309	73E	73F		V	30921	73G	73A	12/62
Ivatt	41310	73E	73F		V	30922	73G	73A	11/61
Ivatt	41311	73E	73F		V	30923	73B	73A	12/62
Ivatt	41312	73E	73F		V	30932	73B	73F	2/61
Ivatt	41313	73E	73F		V	30933	73B	73F	12/61
L1	31753	73H	70A	10/61	V	30934	73B	73F	12/62
L1	31754	73H	70A	11/61	V	30935	73B	73F	12/62
L1	31755	73H	70A	8/59	V	30936	73B	73F	12/62
L1	31756	73F	70A	10/61	V	30937	73B	73F	12/62
L1	31757	73F	70A	12/61	V	30938	73B	73H	7/61
L1	31758	73F	70A	10/59	V	30939	73B	73H	6/61
L1	31759	73F	70A	11/61	N1	31822	73C	73J	11/62
L1	31782	73F	70A	2/61	N1	31876	73C	73J	11/62
L1	31783	73B	70A	11/61	N1	31877	73C	73J	10/62
L1	31784	73B	70A	2/60	N1	31878	73C	73J	10/62
L1	31785	73D	70A	1/60	N1	31879	73C	73J	10/62
L1	31786	73D	70A	2/62	N1	31880	73C	73J	11/62
L1	31787	73D	70A	1/61	WC	34016	73G	73B	6/64
L1	31788	73H	70A	1/60	WC	34017	73G	73B	10/66
L1	31789	73H	70A	11/61	WC	34021	73G	73B	7/67
V	30900	73D	75A	2/62	WC	34022	73G	73B	4/65
V	30901	73D	75A	12/62	WC	34025	73G	73B	7/67
V	30902	73D	70A	12/62	WC	34026	73G	73B	9/66
V	30908	73A	70D	9/61	WC	34027	73G	73B	8/64
V	30909	73A	70A	2/62	WC	34037	73G	73B	7/67
V	30915	73A	75A	12/62	BB	34078	73G	73B	9/64
V	30910	73G	70A	11/61	Cl 2	84025	73G	73F	
V	30911	73G	70A	12/62	Cl 2	84026	73G	73F	

Steam Locomotive Transfers Resulting From KENT COAST ELECTRIFICATION May / June 1959

Class	No	From	To	Withdrawn	Class	No	From	To	Withdrawn
Cl 2	84027	73G	73F		Cl 5	73042		70A	
Cl 2	84028	73G	73F		Cl 5	73080	73A	70A	
Cl 2	84029	73G	73F		Cl 5	73081	73A	70A	
R1	31010	73H	70A	8/59	Cl 5	73082	73A	70A	
R1	31047	73H	70A	3/60	Cl 5	73083	73A	70A	
R1	31174	73H	70A	8/59	Cl 5	73084	73A	70A	
R1	31107	73H	70A	8/59	Cl 5	73085	73A	70A	
R1	31128	73H	70A	8/59	Cl 5	73086	73A	70A	
R1	31337	73H	70A	2/60	Cl 4	75065	73H	71B	
N15	30767	73A	71A	6/59	Cl 4	75066	73H	71B	
N15	30768	73A	71A	10/61	Cl 4	75067	73H	71B	
N15	30769	73A	71A	2/60	Cl 4	75068	73H	71B	
N15	30775	73H	70B	2/60	Cl 4	75069	73H	71B	
N15	30777	73H	70B	10/61	Q1	33001	70C	73J	5/64
N15	30793	73A	70B	8/62	Q1	33003	70C	73J	7/63
N15	30795	73A	70B	7/62	Q1	33003	70C	73J	6/64
N15	30796	73C	72B	2/62	Q1	33004	70C	73J	1/65
N15	30797	73H	72B	6/59	Q1	33014	73C	73J	1/64
N15	30798	73H	72B	6/62	Q1	33037	73C	73J	10/63
N15	30799	73B	72B	3/61	Q1	33039	73C	73J	6/64
N15	30800	73B	71A	8/61	Q1	33040	73C	73J	6/64
N15	30804	73H	71A	7/61					
N15	30805	73H	71A	11/59	70A	Nine Elms			
N15	30806	73C	71A	4/61	70B	Feltham			
MN	35001	73A	70A	11/64	70C	Guildford			
MN	35015	73A	70A	2/64	70D	Basingstoke			
MN	35028	73A	70A	7/67	71A	Eastleigh			
O1	31048	73A	70A	10/60	71B	Bournemouth			
O1	31370	73A	70A	2/60	72A	Exmouth Junction			
Z	30951	73F	72A	11/62	72B	Salisbury			
Z	30952	73F	72A	11/62	73A	Stewarts Lane			
E1	31019	73A	70A to 72B 7/59	4/61	73B	Bricklayers Arms			
E1	31067	73A	70A to 72B 7/59	11/61	73C	Hither Green			
E1	31497	73B	70A to 72B 7/59	10/60	73D	Gillingham (St Leonards)			
E1	31507	73B	70A	7/61	73E	Faversham			
Cl 5	73041		70A		73F	Ashford			

70G   Ramsgate
73H   Dover
73J   Tonbridge
75A   Brighton
75B   Redhill
82F   Weymouth (Until 1959 when became 71G)

Above - *A loose Maunsell 3rd attached to a Bulleid set at Clapham Junction. From 1962 most of the remaining main line Maunsell stock was concentrated on the South Western division but was gradually withdrawn in the years up to 1965.*
Below - *Grove Park to Cannon Street empty Hastings line stock working, seen passing London Bridge behind 'V' 30926 ' Repton'.*

This is the new layout to be installed at the London End of Tonbridge Station: a replacement for the BH track shown on page 94. The new FB inclined layout, (probably 109lb design), is effectively an outside double slip from the Down Slow, with an outside slip beyond on what is the Down Fast, and crossover from Fast to Slow lines including a tandem turnout. By looking at the two pictures it gives a good example of how layouts evolve and receive minor adjustment in the design stage, to use the latest standard components. The normal situation for renewing life expired track is that variations can take place to the p.way, and third rail, provided they are practical and don't alter the principals behind the signal interlocking. Note the right hand track is incomplete. The baseplate position is marked in white paint and the timbers need 'pulling through' to the right which may happen when the layout is transferred to site. The yard is unknown, but could well be Tonbridge. This is the end of the 'ladder' of track which crossed from the Redhill line to the Down side lines connecting various tracks on route.

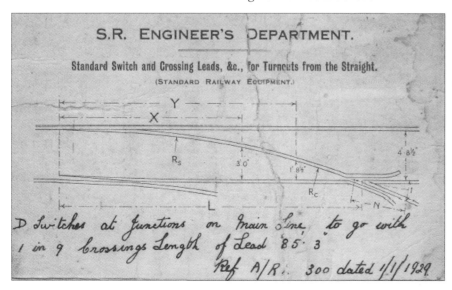

The cover of the small, handy, card S&C standards introduced about 1926, to be applied in future designs for the SR with a note added soon after by a previous owner.

Permanent Way Notes by Graham Hatton

Southern Railway Switch and Crossing Evolution

In the last article I looked at the evolution of plain line and the need for each company to establish standard information for construction and maintenance of track, gauging of structures and clearances. Moving on from that, this article will look the evolution of Switch and Crossing (S&C) standards, from the early days of independent companies into the Southern Railway period. Again I have used early information from the LSWR company simply because I have records of this, but the other companies which later formed the Southern Railway developed along similar lines.

Clearly from the start if you had wanted more than one train on an isolated line you had to develop sidings and hence pointwork. Everything at this stage was, of course, small by later standards and therefore short locomotives and 4-wheel carriages or trucks only required short points. This was just as well because rails were typically only 24ft in length, resulting in numerous joints which precluded being able to make long switches because fishplates in the planed portion of switches and crossing would be impractical. Curve radii could be small, typically just 277ft radius for an LSWR switch (5ft planing) with a 1:5 crossing, as vehicles traversing a crossover and thus reversing in direction were less likely to get the buffers locked. Equally the technology to machine rails at angles to form the finer parts of switches or crossings was not advanced enough to produce more than simple short switches.

By 1880 it appears the LSWR stipulated a minimum radius of 462ft to be used in S&C, though older turnouts would remain for many years in sidings and lesser used routes. This equates to a number 2 switch and 1:7 crossing on the LSWR.

Available space as well as the need to improve a design dictates to a large extent what can be achieved when renewing S&C, and in some cases even today there simply is not the room to improve this radius/angle of crossing. I remember laying an AV 1:6 crossing in at Park Royal in the mid-1970s and there are running junctions with the very tight AV switches in use now 100 years after flatter curves in S&C were recommended. However, this is a good example of a typical early company setting standards in table form to try to achieve desired track formations.

Such switches were straight planed. That is to say the shape of the switch rail end was straight on the machined and running rail sides, from the point toe, to the switch heel beyond the machined limit. Later switches were semi-curved on the running side, curved from the end of the planing to the switch heel (see diagram). This type became the British Standard. Some switches were even fully curved through the planed length on the running side of the switch (GW). The very earliest switches were also 'straight cut', that is to say the back or machined side of the switch was vertical over the rail height and the switch sat in a 'joggle', a formed mis-alignment of the stock rail to give protection from wear, and being struck on the

switch end. However by 1891 when the LSWR produced a new range of turnouts in 82lb double headed rail and 87lb BH (Bullhead Rail) the switches had become undercut. This form allowed a thicker rail near the tip of the switch, with the head of the switch and stock rail being machined to allow the switch to mostly fit under the adjacent stock rail near the tip, to give more strength below the inevitable thin end to a switch (See switch section drawing and picture)

By now rail lengths had also increased to 30ft for the BH style. A joggled switch allowed approximately a depth of 3/8" on each stock rail about 6" in front of the switch in which straight-cut switch tips lay, allowing them to have a bit of thickness at the tip. The gauge is correspondingly increased in this area by this amount. Because of the switches' geometry it was recommended that these switches were used in the facing direction where speed was an issue as they were stronger. Undercut switches referred to above, and used more widely in the 20th century, were recommended for trailing switches. I can remember Salisbury Tunnel Junction having this arrangement until updated to a later standard when re-laid in the 1990s.

Over the years many S&C standards have been set. For instance the LSWR presumably had pre-1891 standards, but so far no recorded evidence has been found of this design, though there must have been manufacturing drawings.

By 1891 they were setting standards for their own rail, as were other companies, and they also used the newer BH rail. By 1902 they produced a new range, for their own 90lb BH rail, still with a 2 ½ inches wide head at this stage. Again in 1908 the range was reviewed and amended for the wider, 2 ¾ inch BH rail then being generally rolled for greater strength.

The rail shape was probably much influenced by the manufacturers who would normally roll rail for more than one company and required 'rolls' specifically suited to each individual rail shape. The final 'roll', to shape the rail when hot, would carry the specific rail details in any roll marks.

The use of different rails, with different head widths in S&C designs, led to the need to alter such items as the planing length of the switches, as the rail became thicker. It also affected the switch radius, but as Peter Bedding says in his excellent and detailed review of S&C of this company for the SW Circle, slavish alterations to the lead lengths (toe to nose) based on mathematical calculation were not made, due presumably, to the cost of producing extensive new drawings and information.

However, things were not to rest there. By the First World War the familiar British Standard BH 95 lb rail (and the lesser-known and soon rejected for S&C layouts 90lb rails) were in wide use and the standard drawings required amendment again, though this time they lasted until the 1923 grouping!

It is worth pointing out that BH refers to a rail shape, rolled in weights from 60 to 100lb per yard in about 5lb in-

TABLE OF LEADS, ETC.

Switch Letter.	Crossing Number. N	Actual Lead Toe of Switch to Nose of Crossing. L	Switch Radius. Rs	Radius of Crossing Curve. Rc	Toe of Switch to 3′ 0″ Offset. X	Toe of Switch to 1′ 8½″ Offset. Y	Crossing Number. N	Switch Letter.
A	5	46′ 11½″	482 ft.	212 ft	27′ 2¼″	37′ 0¾″	5	A
	5½	49′ 0″		264 ,,	27′ 6″	37′ 10½″	5½	
	6	50′ 11¼″		325 ,,	27′ 9½″	39′ 1¾″	6	
	6½	52′ 9½″		396 ,,	28′ 0¼″	40′ 0¾″	6½	
B	7	61′ 1½″	613 ft.	445 ,,	34′ 1¾″	47′ 4¼″	7	B
	7½	63′ 1¾″		524 ,,	34′ 5¾″	48′ 5¼″	7½	
C	8	73′ 5½″	960 ft.	563 ,,	42′ 3″	57′ 7¾″	8	C
	8½	75′ 6¾″		647 ,,	42′ 10½″	58′ 11½″	8½	
	9	77′ 7¼″		740 ,,	42′ 11¾″	59′ 10¾″	9	
	9½	79′ 6¾″		812 ,,	43′ 3½″	60′ 11″	9½	
D	10	89′ 8½″	1,379 ft.	893 ,,	50′ 9″	69′ 11¾″	10	D
	10½	91′ 10″		999 ,,	51′ 4¼″	71′ 2″	10½	
	11	93′ 11″		1,114 ,,	51′ 8″	72′ 3″	11	
	11½	95′ 11¼″		1,239 ,,	52′ 1¼″	73′ 4½″	11½	
E	12	114′ 1¾″	2,446 ft.	1,243 ,,	67′ 0½″	90′ 4½″	12	E
	13	118′ 5½″		1,491 ,,	67′ 9½″	92′ 9″	13	
	14	122′ 7½″		1,771 ,,	68′ 6¾″	95′ 0¼″	14	
	15	126′ 7″		2,087 ,,	69′ 2½″	97′ 1½″	15	
F	16	151′ 3¼″	3,768 ft.	2,253 ,,	88′ 10¾″	119′ 7½″	16	F
	17	155′ 5¾″		2,591 ,,	89′ 8½″	121′ 11½″	17	
	18	159′ 6¾″		2,963 ,,	90′ 4½″	124′ 1½″	18	
	20	168′ 5½″		3,770 ,,	93′ 9¼″	130′ 4″	20	

Alternative Leads for use where the above cannot be adopted.

Switch Letter.	N	L	Rs	Rc	X	Y	N	Switch Letter.
A	7	54′ 5″	482 ft.	480 ft.	28′ 1½″	40′ 9½″	7	A
B	8	65′ 1¼″	613 ,,	612 ,,	34′ 10″	49′ 5¾″	8	B
C	10	81′ 5″	960 ,,	956 ,,	43′ 6½″	61′ 10¼″	10	C
D	12	97′ 8½″	1,379 ,,	1,379 ,,	52′ 3½″	74′ 3″	12	D
E	16	130′ 3¾″	2,446 ,,	2,449 ,,	69′ 8½″	98′ 11¾″	16	E

NOTES.—It is important that Switches and Crossings should not be combined otherwise than as shown above. For turnouts from curves, the particulars will be supplied by the Divisional Engineers.

CHIEF ENGINEER'S OFFICE,
WATERLOO STATION.

JUNE, 1926.

creasing steps. It is not all 95lb rail though, although this was certainly very common in this country.

By World War 1 the railway companies had to share more common standards in many aspects, so the Railway Engineering Association (REA) produced requirements which most railway companies adopted. The LSWR along with other companies, started the process of redrawing the S&C standard components and this was finished by the new Southern Railway with a suite of new drawings and charts issued in 1926. Thereafter things rested for many years until World War 2 when the American FB (Flat Bottom) Rails were tried. 98 lb, 109lb, 110A and 113 rails were tried in the years 1936 to 1940 and eventually in 1948 the new British Railways adopted a purpose-designed 113A rail, though miles of the three last of the above still exist. There never was a finalised 98lb S&C design, as it was considered the rail was not strong enough vertically, at virtually the same height as BH rail, but a new design was issued for 109lb S&C after the war and its dimensions were very similar to REA BH in lead length etc.

The above has briefly referred to the development of switches and turnouts. Early crossings used in these turnouts were short and had sharp angles, 1:5 to 1:8 being common until the 1880s. The angle, measured as a ratio of the opening between the two crossing rails of one unit, compared to the distance from the theoretical intersection of those two rails in 'x' units, hence 1: 'x' units. (note this theoretical intersection is slightly in advance of the actual manufactured and slightly rounded crossing nose, see diagram). Crossings became flatter as the need for a larger radius to the turnout to accommodate higher speeds developed, so 1:7 crossings as mentioned above became the normal sharpest crossing with values of 1:20 being included in the 1902 LSWR standards for higher speed turnouts, or heavily curved adapted turnouts.

Wing rails and check rails also evolved with these crossings. In the early days with low speeds the check-rail and crossing wing-rail ends could be rounded. The wheel flange would strike it slowly if at all and needed little leading into the correct lateral path through the crossing area, though the 'ride' through pointwork on trains must have been very poor. It was soon appreciated that a flared end to check-rails would need to be used to allow the wheel flange a more gentle adjustment at speed to the correct position to pass through the crossing and check-rail gap. So in the 1902 standards this item was specifically upgraded. No more were the rounded check-rail ends to be used.

So certainly from the late 19th century, S&C standards were laid down in tables for adoption in designs and standard turnouts produced in drawing form for detail of chair position and type to be identified. To the drawing office the drawings would be immensely useful showing detail which could be adapted, but to the man on the ground if he was required to build a turnout from supplied material, which was still common practice for very simple layouts, he would find the tables of most use, giving key dimensions and utilising standard supplied components, all of which had originally been developed as a total concept.

As said above, in 1926 the SR produced a book of drawings, each drawing featuring a particular switch or crossing element. Within the standards there were also drawings of double and single slips, typical timbering of layouts and the specialist chairs associated with S&C etc. They were beautifully drawn and reproduced at about 3ft x 2ft with each chair and bolt shown and identified along with the dimensions between timbers, rail lengths, angles and all critical dimensions. These drawings were not designed for site use, but intended for laying the 'building blocks' of standard items for adoption in simple layouts , or adaptation to more complex ones by the drawing office.

To give some examples, crossings used a set chair sequence which would have the crossing angle involved cast on the appropriate chair as well as the chair's identity. All crossings called the nose chair A. This chair was slightly offset to allow for a nose holding-down bolt and consisted of a 1 ¾" mild steel plate and brackets all bolted down with blocks and a through bolt through the crossing nose to hold it all together. The next chairs holding the splice and point rails or 'Vee' of the crossing being B, C, D chairs as required etc., each chair being unique to a specific angle, or a small range of angles. In

Opposite page -
The inside of the same card Switch and Crossing standards issued by the new SR and the columns that relate to the front drawing in the previous photo.

Right - *Two extracted pages from the large 2 x3 ft plan book that was issued by the SR in 1926 to accompany the then new standards for Bullhead Track. These two sheets give a flavour of the contents and show the standard switch arrangement for A and B straightcut switches. These would then be adapted by the drawing office to a specific site if reqd. There is a lot of detail on these drawings, but the switch rails themselves had separate manufacturing drawings to show all the planing detail. The second example shows the detail for the centre of a 1:8 double slip. Note the special 'slab and bracket' chairs either side of the mid obtuse crossing point and the through bolt from one side of this chair to the other holding all the rails blocks and brackets together. In addition it shows the use of the square shaped, but less space consuming L1 chairs.*

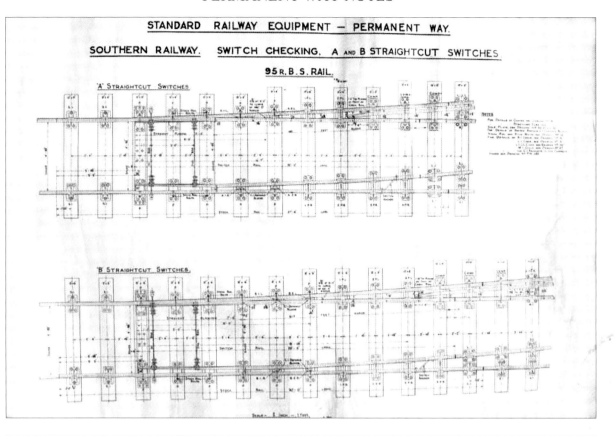

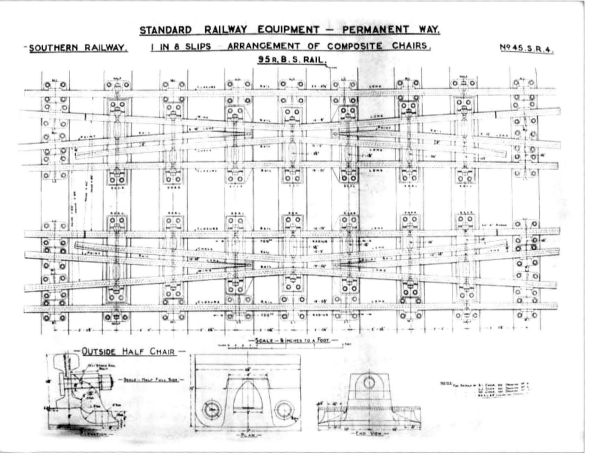

The London end of Tonbridge Station with the Down Slow to the left of the platform and the Down Bay to the right. It clearly shows the 'Ladder' arrangement from the Redhill Line which gave access from this route. The longer outside slip switches allowed a better ride through the slip switches at a faster speed. The new layout which replaced this BH design moved the track marginally towards London, but probably slightly sharpened the angle of the crossing from the Redhill Line to the Sevenoaks Line. Outside slips would have helped by being less restricting to an alteration to the angle of the two routes. The old layout was mechanically worked, the new layout appeared to be converted to motor operation. Changes in the lever frame including shortening the levers to indicate that less force was needed to them, and electrical switching for the motor from the lever tail would have been made during the work.

front of the crossing the chairs were X nearest, then Y and Z if required. The use of smaller square-based chairs such as L1 with ordinary S1s allowed the number of specialist chairs to be kept to a minimum.

The vast majority of these chairs then sat on 12" x 6" timbers at 2'6" centres. The wing-rails had a total length of 12'3" for crossings 1:6 to 1:10 ½: this includes the splay beyond the crossing nose. With these crossings 10'7 ½ " splice rails with 11'7" point rails for 1:6 and 1:6 ½ crossings, and 13'1 ½" and 14'1" rails respectively for 1:7 to 1:11 crossings were used. It is generally known that all rails were at this stage inclined inwards to match the wheels 'coning' at an angle of 1:20. However in order to simplify the machining, the match of the splice rail and point rail (this is the rail in which the crossing nose is formed) was actually made vertically from the nose to the heel or back of the splice of the two rails. Thereafter the rails were slowly inclined to the 1:20 angle over the next couple of chairs. The chairs under the crossing allowed for this alteration of rail verticality. Check-rails to crossings were also vertical in this standard.

Switches too used standard components. All used P chairs, the slide chair, and the slightly longer slide 1P and 2P chairs towards the heel of the switches, with 3P to 11P chairs beyond this with both rails fixed according to the type of switch. Timber spacing varied from about 2'4" to 2'6" centres. Beyond the P chair all chairs were 'handed' Left or Right. 'A'

straightcut switches for instance used five P chairs then, 1P, 2P, 3P, 4P and two L1 chairs. 'B' straightcut switches used one more P chair position.

In the SR standard drawings the switches ranged from A to F with corresponding crossings from 1:5 to 1:20. At this stage it is worth pointing out that the beloved B switch with a 1:8 crossing was not considered the best match. B switches went with 1:7 and 1:7 ½ crossings. The C switch covering from 1:8 to 1: 9½ crossings. However in a further small table at the bottom it was allowed to use a B switch where the above could not be easily adopted, though it does not say where this was to apply!

In very small print it made clear that the above was all that was allowed without the Divisional Engineer's approval! The local Supervisor was not allowed to invent his own solutions! To help clarify the requirements some companies also took this a stage further and produced small-scale standard turnout drawings. The GW had these for their track turnouts, though they had gone their own way on some items such as switches, and not fully adopted the REA design recommendations in 1923.

The SR, keen to provide information to their front line staff, produced a booklet in card in 1926 of 'Standard Switch and Crossing Leads for Turnouts from the Straight' to give basic information taken from the bigger standard drawings.

In a separate article I will attempt to show how the

standards can be adopted for turnouts on curves with cant etc. as clearly not all S&C can ever be accommodated on straight track: also a little more on switch components. Nevertheless the above system of standards laid down ground rules and components which could be adopted, and almost all layouts, no matter how complex, were made using these standard switches and crossing components and still are today.

References used:-

LSWR Switches and Crossings in the SW Circle Literature. April 1999 by Peter Bedding. (Date incorrectly listed in last literature).
LSWR Standard Switch and Crossing Drawings.
Railway Permanent Way published in 1922.
British Railway Track, Design, Construction and Maintenance, 1st,2nd, and 4th editions, by the Permanent Way Institute.
Southern Railway Handbook, Instruction to Engineering Department Staff 1926 & 1936.
Southern Railway, Standard Railway Equipment (P.Way) 95RBS Switches and Crossing Drawings 1926.

LSWR SWITCH AND CROSSING DATA 1902 DESIGN

Switch No	Xing Angle.	Switch planning	Switch length	Switch Radius	Radius of xing curve.	Length toe to 1' 8 1/2"offset	Length toe to nose.
	N	length in feet	length in feet	Rad. in feet	Rad. in feet	Feet	Feet
1	5	5' 8 1/2"	30' 00"	312	220	26' 2 1/2"	45' 8"
	5 1/2	"	"	"	267	26' 10 3/4"	48' 0 1/2"
2	6	7' 0"	"	470	319	32' 0 1/4"	55' 3 3/4"
	6 1/2	"	"	"	374	32' 9 1/4"	57' 11 3/4"
	7	"	"	"	435	33' 0 1/2"	59' 7 1/2"
3	7 1/2	8' 7 1/2"	"	709	500	39' 8"	68' 8 1/2"
	8	"	"	"	568	40' 4 1/2 "	71' 3 3/4"
	8 1/2	"	"	"	642	40' 7"	73 1 1/2"
4	9	10' 6 1/2"	"	1065	720	48' 3 3/4"	83' 1 1/2"
	9 1/2	"	"	"	803	49' 2"	85' 11"
	10	"	"	"	889	49' 7 1/2"	88' 3 1/2"
	10 1/2	"	"	"	980	49' 9"	89' 10"
5	11	12' 11"	"	1600	1076	59' 2 1/2"	101' 8 1/2"
	11 1/2	"	"	"	1177	60' 1"	104' 6 3/4"
	12	"	"	"	1282	60' 8 3/4"	107' 1 1/4"
	13	"	"	"	1505	61' 0"	110' 3 1/4"
6	14	15' 10"	45' 00"	2409	1745	73' 7 3/4"	127' 8 3/4"
	15	"	"	"	2004	74' 9"	132' 8 1/4"
	16	"	"	"	2280	74' 10 1/4"	135' 4 1/2"
7	17	19' 10"	"	3768	2575	91' 2 1/4"	156' 10"
	18	"	"	"	2887	92' 10 1/4"	162' 4"
	20	"	"	"	3564	93' 7 1/2"	169' 2 3/4"

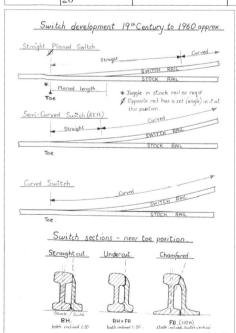

Notes:

The above table was designed for use with 2 1/2", 90lb rail.

The change from the switch radius to the radius of the crossing occurred close to the 1' 8 1/2" opening.

The switch was straight over its planed length and met the stock rail at fixed angle.

The switch curve if continued towards the toe would be parrallel to the through straight 3" inside the stock rail.

First fixed chair at heel of switch, for a No.2 switch 19'11" from the toe.

The position of the switch toe was 3" beyond the centre of the timber it rested on increasing the switch toe support.

Wing rails for 1:5 to 1:9 1/2 crossings were held in the nose chair and two beyond it. The check rail was 10' 6" long.

Wing rails for 1:10 to 1:20 crossings were held in the nose chair and three beyond it. The check rail was 13ft long.in 5 chairs.

The above switches were semi curved. That is straight to the end of the planing length. Note the end of the switch rail.

The LSWR produced an earlier table of Turnout dimensions about 1891 for the rails in use at that time. These switches had straight planing.

- in spring a young's man thoughts turn to.........

..........SNOW PLOUGHS of course- !?!?*!!*!

Adverse weather conditions, be that autumn leaf fall or extremes of temperature have long been the bane of the operators life. The media especially quick to jump on the band-wagon when a particular railway engineer was heard to comment over, '...the wrong type of snow'.

To be fair, the Southern Region has never been as regularly or indeed severely affected as other railways, although this in itself may create its own problems as there is then the necessary decision to be made over investing in potentially expensive equipment that might well stand idle for 51 weeks of the year.

The subject of snow clearance is one we may well return to in more detail later (note I deliberately did not say " with a flurry"), but all joking apart, the decision also had to be made as the winter approached, whether to make a ready a locomotive(s) which would then remain on stand-by for long periods unable also to perform any other useful work.

In steam days this was often the chosen practice, an 0-6-0, usually a '700' or 'Q' being permanently allocated to such duties although west of Exeter it has been said a Maunsell Mogul would perform a similar task - *any pictures please?* Two engines so prepared might then be coupled either end of a brake van, the latter provided for tools, equipment and of course men. In the top view a 'C' class 0-6-0 in singular guise was recorded at Brighton on 16 March 1958.

With steam power being slowly rendered extinct, the operating department cast around for an alternative, a large angular fitting clearly not considered suitable on the front end of a diesel or electric locomotive, although some diesel classes did of course carry small shields intended to act as ploughs.

The more appropriate option was an independent plough which might then be propelled. Thus it was that in 1964/65 Eastleigh Works converted eight tenders from former 'Schools' class locomotives which remained 'in service' until the 1990s. (A number of tenders from former 'V2' type locomotives were similarly converted for the LMR at the same time.) Several of the former have survived into preservation although most are intended to form the basis of a reversion to conventional tenders for use behind preserved locomotives. For more information, the reader is directed to the website http://www.maunsell.org.uk/present%20project/tenders.htm

Photographs, top - G W Sharpe.
Bottom - Salisbury 20 July 1967,
J H Aston

COLOUR INTERLUDE

Page 97 - A wonderfully 'moody' image taken in Southampton Docks - contributed with thanks.

Opposite page - Two rather grainy images of 34107 at the time it carried the simple name of 'Blandford'. But look at the sand-fillers, definitely non standard!   *The John Knottley collection, courtesy of The Swanage Railway Trust*

Above - 'Green on Green' at Swanage. Paul Hersey collection.

Bottom - Finally in this potpourri of material, weed-killing at the top end of the east yard at Eastleigh, Allbrook signal box is in the background.

A taster on the delights of what can be expected in Issue 11 on Crawley.......you have been warned.

Paul Hersey collection